# Department for \
# Departmental Re



Presented to Parliament by the Secretary of State for Work and Pensions and the Chief Secretary to the Treasury by Command of Her Majesty
May 2006

Cm 6829 £42.00

# CONTENTS

## Table of Figures

# FOREWORD

**Building a fair society which promotes opportunity and independence for all lies at the heart of our vision for Britain. This is a high aspiration, and the targets which we are working towards are rightly some of the most demanding that any Government has ever set itself.**

This report sets out our progress towards these long-term goals. It shows how our reforms of welfare and pensions are making a difference in tackling poverty and worklessness, and in enabling people to take control of their retirement planning. It also highlights the practical improvements we are making now to offer a better quality of service to the seventeen million customers who rely on us. We are redesigning our system of child support in Britain, and in the interim period we are streamlining processes in the Child Support Agency to deliver more money for more children. This year the number of integrated Jobcentre Plus offices in operation has risen above seven hundred, and the number of people who have entered employment through the Pathways to Work programme has topped seventeen thousand. We are making it easier for pensioners to claim the benefits they are entitled to; we are ahead of our target to cut the processing time for a claim for Housing Benefit; overpayments in Income Support and Jobseeker's Allowance have almost halved since 1997-98; and fraud is at its lowest ever.

These changes have driven significant progress. We've made the biggest improvement of any EU country in tackling child poverty. There are more people in jobs than ever before – 2.4 million more than in 1997. And we've lifted two million pensioners out of absolute poverty. Last year's Disability Discrimination Act set a new standard in disability rights, and with the establishment of the Office for Disability Issues we're now focused on improving outcomes for disabled people.

We have achieved a great deal in the past year, but we will need to redouble our efforts to meet the challenging targets that are outlined in this report. This year's Welfare Reform Green Paper *A New Deal for Welfare; Empowering People to Work* set out our vision of an enabling and empowering welfare state. Meanwhile our National Pensions Debate engaged and challenged the public on the crucial issue of retirement provision, and now we are preparing to publish a White Paper on our plans for fundamental reform of the pensions system in the UK.

We could not have made the progress set out in this document – and we could not expect to build on and to exceed these achievements in coming years – without the continued hard work of all of our staff. I'd like to thank them on behalf of my ministerial team for their commitment and professionalism.

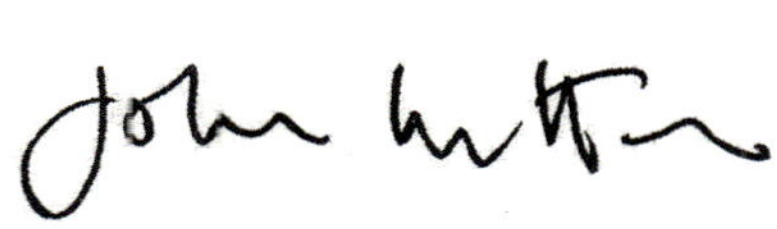

**John Hutton**
Secretary of State for Work and Pensions

# THE DEPARTMENT'S MINISTERS

**The Right Honourable John Hutton MP**
Secretary of State for Work and Pensions

**Jim Murphy MP**
Minister for Employment and Welfare Reform

**James Purnell MP**
Minister for Pensions Reform

**James Plaskitt MP**
Parliamentary Under Secretary (Commons)

**Lord Hunt of Kings Health OBE**
Parliamentary Under Secretary (Lords)

**Anne McGuire MP**
Parliamentary Under Secretary (Commons) and Minister for Disabled People

# 01 INTRODUCTION AND OVERVIEW

# WHAT DO WE DO?

## The Department for Work and Pensions provides opportunities for millions of people.

We enable people to find jobs, help children out of poverty, support those out of work, provide security in retirement, strive to advance the rights of disabled people and improve health and safety in the workplace.

Here are a few examples of what we have been doing to meet our objectives in 2005–06.

"The UK employment rate is one of the highest of the G7 group of industrialised countries."

# WORK

## KEY EVENTS

- Publication of the Welfare Reform Green Paper set out a radical series of welfare reforms to enable people to escape poverty, fulfil their potential and strengthen their independence by coming off benefit and moving into work.
- More than 700 new integrated Jobcentre Plus offices were rolled out across the country.
- Pathways to Work, a scheme offering more help to Incapacity Benefit customers, expanded to 14 more Jobcentre Plus districts.
- An enhanced lone parent programme – New Deal Plus for Lone Parents — was piloted in five Jobcentre Plus Districts.

## OUR OBJECTIVE

**"Promote work as the best form of welfare for people of working age, while protecting the position of those in greatest need."**

"We are committed to ensuring parents meet their financial responsibilities to their children – the Child Support Agency deals with over 1 million cases a year and last year collected around £600 million for children."

# CHILDREN

## KEY EVENTS

- The Child Support Agency launched an Operational Improvement Plan to ensure more effective collection and payment of child support.
- Sir David Henshaw tasked with carrying out a fundamental redesign of child support.
- Significant progress made towards eradicating child poverty.
- DWP worked with the Department for Education and Skills to implement a national strategy to increase access to childcare.

## OUR OBJECTIVE

**"Ensure the best start for all children and end child poverty by 2020."**

"2.7 million households are now receiving Pension Credit."

# PENSIONS

## KEY EVENTS

- The National Pensions Debate – a national consultation culminating in National Pensions Day – achieved major success in building a consensus on pension reform.
- The Pension Commission, led by Lord Turner, published two key reports, helping to push the debate forward.
- Pension Credit take-up increased after a direct mail initiative – "You're Missing Out" – targeted 1.5m people identified by data matching as most likely to be missing out on Pension Credit.

## OUR OBJECTIVE

**"Combat poverty and promote security and independence in retirement for today's and tomorrow's pensioners."**

"The employment rate of disabled people is going up…the gap between the overall employment rate and the employment rate of disabled people is going down."

# DISABILITY

## KEY EVENTS

- The Disability Discrimination Act extended the rights of disabled people.
- A 20-year strategy –Improving the Life Chances of Disabled People – was launched.
- A new Office for Disability Issues was established.

## OUR OBJECTIVE

**"Improve rights and opportunities for disabled people in a fair and inclusive society."**

**"Fraud is at its lowest ever level."**

# FRAUD

## KEY EVENTS

- A 44 percent reduction in fraud and error in Income Support and Jobseeker's Allowance.
- An Official Error Task Force set up to cut losses to the taxpayer.

## OUR OBJECTIVE

**"Ensure customers receive a high quality service."**

**"HSE aims to achieve a record of workplace health and safety that leads the world."**

# HEALTH AND SAFETY

## KEY EVENTS

- DWP, the Department of Health, and the Health and Safety Executive (HSE), jointly launched a new strategy to improve the health and well-being of people of working age.
- HSE developed and launched stress management standards to help businesses manage work-related stress better.
- Occupational health advice – Workplace Health Connect – provided to small and medium sized enterprises across England and Wales.

## OUR OBJECTIVE

**"By 2008 improve health and safety outcomes in Great Britain through progressive improvement in the control of risk in the workplace."**

**We make the best use of technology to deliver our services...**

We have invested around **2.8 billion** in modern IT infrastructure in the past few years.

We have around **8,000** touch screen 'job point' terminals.

**400,000** job vacancies currently available on the internet at **www.jobcentreplus.gov.uk** – the Government's single most popular online service.

More than **97 per cent** of benefit accounts are now paid directly into bank or building society accounts meaning reduced fraud and less costs to the taxpayer.

**...but nothing could happen without the commitment of our staff who make sure the customer always comes first.**

"Every person is an individual – that's what you have to remember. I get the most satisfaction out of seeing the change in the lone parents who come to see me. They arrive for their first New Deal interview, unsure and nervous, and the change when someone comes in saying "Mandy, I've got a job" is unbelievable."

**Mandy Grant, New Deal for Lone Parents Adviser, Jobcentre Plus in Edinburgh**

"It's really satisfying when a customer you've helped comes back to thank you. For example, I was dealing with a customer who wanted to go on a training course. I was able to advise the customer and point him in the direction of other providers who might be able to help with funding. Only recently he popped his head round the door to tell me my advice had worked. He'd got the funding he needed and was that much closer to getting a job!"

**Mike Woodrow is an Incapacity Benefit Personal Adviser for Jobcentre Plus in Wales.**

# OUR VALUES

**We aim to deliver the best possible service for the people who rely on us. That's why our four Values are: Achieving the Best, Making a Difference, Respecting People and Looking Outwards.**

**But what do the people we help think of our work?**

"I'm so glad I applied for Pension Credit. It has made a tremendous difference to me. I get around so much easier now because when I'm not feeling well I can afford to take a taxi."

**Eugenie Hobbs, age 83**

"I spent a year unable to work, dependent on Incapacity Benefit but I could see working in childcare as a solution to my employment problem. I called into Biggleswade Jobcentre Plus and had a meeting with my advisor Diane Welham. She was very supportive and provided me with lots of information about organisations that could help."

**Gary Powers, age 41**

"I had been on Income Support for 13 years and as I was on my own with two young children. I thought there was no way to improve our lives. I made an appointment at the Jobcentre in Leyland, and went to meet Barbara, who helps lone parents. The very next day Barbara phoned and said that a job had just come in. Getting my first wage was brilliant."

**Denise Nicholson**

# 2005–06: THE HIGHLIGHTS

A **44 per cent reduction** in fraud and error in Income Support and Jobseeker's Allowance since 1997.

Expanded Pathways to Work for Incapacity Benefit customers to **14** more Jobcentre Plus districts and over **21,000** customers into work, so far.

For the first time more than a **million** lone parents in employment.

More than **2.7 million** Automatic State Pension Forecasts were issued.

Child Support Agency staff answered **more calls** more quickly.

The Disability Living Allowance/Attendance Allowance national telephone service **achieved** the Call Centre Association Standards Council **accreditation**.

DWP Diversity policies awarded the **Gold standard** from the Race for Opportunity benchmarking exercise.

A campaign made **small** and **medium-sized enterprises** aware of their obligations under the Disability Discrimination Act.

New stress management standards were **launched** to **help** businesses manage work-related stress better.

# WE'RE GETTING THERE

## We know that we still need to improve in a number of areas. That's why:

We've introduced an Operational Improvement Plan for the Child Support Agency which will bring about more effective collection and payment

We've set up an Error Task Force to address the level of error in the benefit system.

We're modernising our IT – bringing it up to scratch in those areas where it still lets staff down.

We're using contact centre technology to make The Pension Service more efficient.

# OUR VISION FOR THE FUTURE

## A welfare state that supports people to move on and escape poverty rather than consigning them to a life on benefits.

A welfare state that provides an accessible service based around the needs of customers and supports people in what they can do rather than what they can't.

A welfare state that gives people more choices to work longer if they want to and safeguards their pension provision.

# GETTING THERE

**We have pledged to deliver an annual five per cent real-terms reduction from 2008-09 to 2010-11 across our administrative and programme budgets plus capital.**

This means there are likely to be some further changes in the Department including staff reductions beyond 2007-08.

However, we now have the certainty to develop detailed plans to take us forward into the next decade.

We will develop a capable and flexible workforce with the skills and capabilities to meet current and future business requirements.

We will develop a performance culture where performance is valued, delivered, recognised and customer-focused

We will develop leadership capabilities resulting in inspirational and effective leaders with the capability and confidence to lead through transformational change.

# 02 THE DEPARTMENT'S OBJECTIVES AND STRATEGY

# AIM AND OBJECTIVES

THE DEPARTMENT FOR WORK AND PENSIONS EXISTS TO **PROMOTE OPPORTUNITY AND INDEPENDENCE FOR ALL**. IT PROVIDES HELP TO INDIVIDUALS AND SUPPORTS THE COUNTRY'S ECONOMIC GROWTH AND SOCIAL COHESION.

THE DEPARTMENT HELPS INDIVIDUALS TO ACHIEVE THEIR POTENTIAL THROUGH EMPLOYMENT, TO PROVIDE FOR THEMSELVES, THEIR CHILDREN AND THEIR FUTURE RETIREMENT. IT WORKS WITH OTHERS TO COMBAT POVERTY, BOTH OF ASPIRATION AND OUTCOME.

**1.** To support this aim, the Department has a number of strategic objectives which aim to:

- ensure the best start for all children and end child poverty by 2020;
- promote work as the best form of welfare for people of working age[1], while protecting the position of those in greatest need;
- combat poverty and promote security and independence in retirement for today's and tomorrow's pensioners;
- improve rights and opportunities for disabled people in a fair and inclusive society; and
- ensure customers receive a high quality service, including high levels of accuracy.

**2.** These objectives are underpinned by the Department's Public Service Agreement which sets out specific targets that must be met.

## The Department's strategy

**3.** To achieve a fairer and more inclusive society, the Government is moving further away from a passive welfare system to one which encourages the development of potential and supports its realisation across people's lives. This entails a preventative approach to social problems which involves supporting people to develop skills and financial assets, and to manage their health conditions throughout their lives.

**4.** Tackling the medium- and longer-term challenges facing society requires close working between this and other government departments, employers, healthcare providers, those providing opportunity through education and skills, as well as other stakeholders across the economic and social sectors.

**5.** The Department recognises that it needs to support people to achieve the best possible outcomes for themselves over the course of longer, active lives. For the individual, outcomes are largely determined by experiences in earlier periods of their life.

**1** The Department's employment programmes and many of its initiatives do not have specific upper age eligibility limits. This recognises that people will increasingly wish to work up to age 65 and beyond.

For example:

- where parents, particularly lone parents, are out of work for prolonged periods, it increases the probability of poverty for their children;
- childhood poverty is a predictor of less successful outcomes in adult life, including inactivity and unemployment; and
- a pensioner's retirement income is determined by patterns of working and saving during their working life.

**6.** The Department's approach to supporting its customers across the lifecycle was set out in its Five Year Strategy *Opportunity and security throughout life* (Cm 6447 February 2005)[2] and comprises the following key elements:

- more people in work, choosing to work longer and save more;
- supporting families and children; and
- security and dignity in retirement.

**7.** Equality for disabled people supports successful outcomes at each stage in the lifecycle.

### Main elements of the Department's strategy

**8.** The benefits of **work** – for individuals, families and society – are clear. Work is the surest way out of poverty and towards greater independence and inclusion. It is also the only way to meet the challenges of an ageing, and increasingly globalised society.

**9.** The success of the Government's welfare to work reforms has been within a clear framework of rights and responsibilities, matching a strong economy with an enabling welfare state. In particular this has meant enhancing support for the unemployed through Jobcentre Plus and the New Deals, while extending employment policies for those traditionally seen as outside the labour market, like lone parents and those on incapacity benefits.

In the last year, the Department has:

- continued the rollout of Jobcentre Plus with over 700 fully integrated offices in operation, ensuring that everyone benefits from the improved support offered;
- further refined the Jobseeker's Allowance regime, including piloting alternative approaches to delivery. Research shows that regular, frequent face-to-face contact is essential to helping people back to work, and that sanctions provide critical reinforcement of the rights and responsibilities agenda;
- continued to make work possible and make work pay for lone parents. Work-focused interviews and the New Deal for Lone Parents have been extended, with further support through the National Childcare Strategy, Minimum Wage and Tax Credits. The Department is continuing to build on its success by piloting financial measures to assist with work search and provide in-work support;

2 www.dwp.gov.uk/publications/dwp/2005/5_yr_strat/index.asp

- begun testing new ways of using public procurement to promote race equality, and extending outreach services for ethnic minorities, focused on non-working partners in low income households in the cities with the highest ethnic minority populations (to be delivered by Jobcentre Plus);

- extended its Pathways to Work programme for people with health conditions and disabilities. Early evidence is encouraging, with an increase of around eight percentage points in the number leaving benefits in the first six months of their claim. The Department has also continued its current employment programmes for disabled people including New Deal for Disabled People; Workstep; Remploy; Access to Work; and Workprep; and

- launched a National Guidance Campaign in May 2005 to enhance employers' awareness of, and ability to adopt, non-ageist practices such as flexible employment and retirement opportunities to improve the recruitment, training and retention of older workers.

**10.** More needs to be done to provide a welfare state that enables people to escape poverty and long-term dependency. The Green Paper *A New Deal for Welfare: Empowering People to Work*[3] sets out how the Department will build on its success and make progress towards the long-term aim of an employment rate equivalent to 80 per cent of the working-age population.

**11.** To support **families and children**, the Department's strategy is to:

- extend the work-focused interview programme by introducing mandatory action plans for all lone parents, and quarterly work-focused interviews for those lone parents with children aged 14 and over;

- pilot New Deal Plus for Lone Parents in five Jobcentre Plus Districts from April 2005, bringing together the existing pilots (including Worksearch Premium, In-work Credit and Extended School Childcare), supported by a range of other measures into a coherent package of support to enhance the existing New Deal for Lone Parents/ work-focused interviews model and encourage more lone parents to participate in the New Deal. A further two pilots, one in Scotland and one in Wales, are planned from October 2006;

- through the 10 Year Childcare Strategy, provide good quality, affordable, flexible early education and childcare, which meets the needs of working parents, for children between the ages of 3 and 14 years. To support this aim the Government is putting in place a network of 3,500 Sure Start Children's Centres for pre-school children by 2010, and Extended Schools for school-age children; and

**Work is the surest way out of poverty and towards greater independence and inclusion.**

3 www.dwp.gov.uk/aboutus/welfarereform/

- implement the Child Support Agency's Operational Improvement Plan to improve the Agency's performance while work to redesign future policy and delivery arrangements is undertaken.

**12.** For **pensioners**, the Department's strategy is to:

- tackle pensioner poverty by increasing the take-up of Pension Credit and working with partners to help pensioners access the full range of financial and other help available to them;
- improve the security of, and bolster confidence in, private pensions, to enable people to make informed choices about their retirement, and provide opportunities for a more flexible retirement;
- drive forward effective pensions protection and regulation, building on the foundations of the Pensions Act 2004 through the Pension Protection Fund, the Financial Assistance Scheme and the Pensions Regulator; and
- promote individual responsibility and raise awareness of pension provision among people of working age through the Informed Choice programme.

**13.** The Pensions Commission, led by Lord Turner of Echinswell, was established following the Government's Pensions Green Paper in 2002 to review the UK private pension system and long-term savings, and make recommendations for change. The Commission delivered its second report[4] in November 2005.

**14.** It highlighted the challenge posed by increasing life expectancies and the need for people to save more to provide security for their retirement. In addition, the Pensions Commission analysis underlined the importance of the measures already being promoted to give individuals the choice as well as the opportunity to stay in work longer.

**15.** To raise awareness of the choices ahead and to build as broad a consensus as possible around the way forward, the Department launched the National Pensions debate, culminating in National Pensions Day on 18 March, when over 1,000 people across the UK took part in a deliberative discussion on the pensions challenge and the Commission's options for reform. The Government will shortly set out its response to the Commission's recommendations in a White Paper.

**16.** To improve rights and opportunities for **disabled people**, the Department's strategy is to:

- implement the provisions of the Disability Discrimination Act 2005 and take forward related work to deliver enhanced civil rights for disabled people, including sponsoring the Disability Rights Commission and ensuring that institutional support for disability rights will be maintained in the planned Commission for Equality and Human Rights;
- drive forward the long-term, cross-government programme of work to improve outcomes for disabled people, including implementing the recommendations of the Strategy Unit report *Improving the Life Chances of Disabled People*[5];and

**4** www.pensionscommission.org.uk
**5** www.strategy.gov.uk/work_areas/disability/

- create new mechanisms for involving disabled people throughout the policy making and service delivery process.

**17.** To ensure customers receive a **high-quality service**, the Department's strategy is to:

- move to more efficient ways of communicating, transform the Department's operations, continue to tackle fraud and error, and simplify the benefit system;
- make changes to the Child Support Agency's structure and processes to bring about reductions in uncleared cases, faster clearance of applications and increased levels of compliance;
- introduce significant improvements in the administration of Housing Benefit and the way in which the Department works with local authorities;
- improve the quality of service and reduce the complexity of claiming benefits by:
  - tailoring its services to its customers so that it is able to provide the right level of support for their needs;
  - supporting its staff to deliver performance at higher levels of productivity; and
  - transforming its supporting operations to be as effective and efficient as possible.

**Simplifying the Benefits System**

**18.** The Department accepts the need for a simpler, more transparent benefit system that makes it easier for customers to access the support they need when their circumstances change, and to help them move on and into work where they can.

**19.** As announced in the Five Year Strategy, the Department is exploring and developing ways to tackle benefit complexity while continuing to protect social security expenditure. In doing so, the intention is to continue providing the best support for helping people into work while protecting the position of those in greatest need. This difficult balance was recognised by the National Audit Office in its report *Dealing with the complexity of the benefits system*[6], published on 18 November 2005, which equally acknowledged that the Department has already taken a number of steps to tackle complexity.

**20.** In response to the report the Department has, in addition, established a Benefit Simplification Unit to focus and take forward its efforts to simplify the benefit system.

**The Government is considering its response to the Commission's recommendations and will set out its proposals for reform in a White Paper later in the spring.**

6 www.nao.org.uk/publications/nao_reports/05-06/0506592.pdf

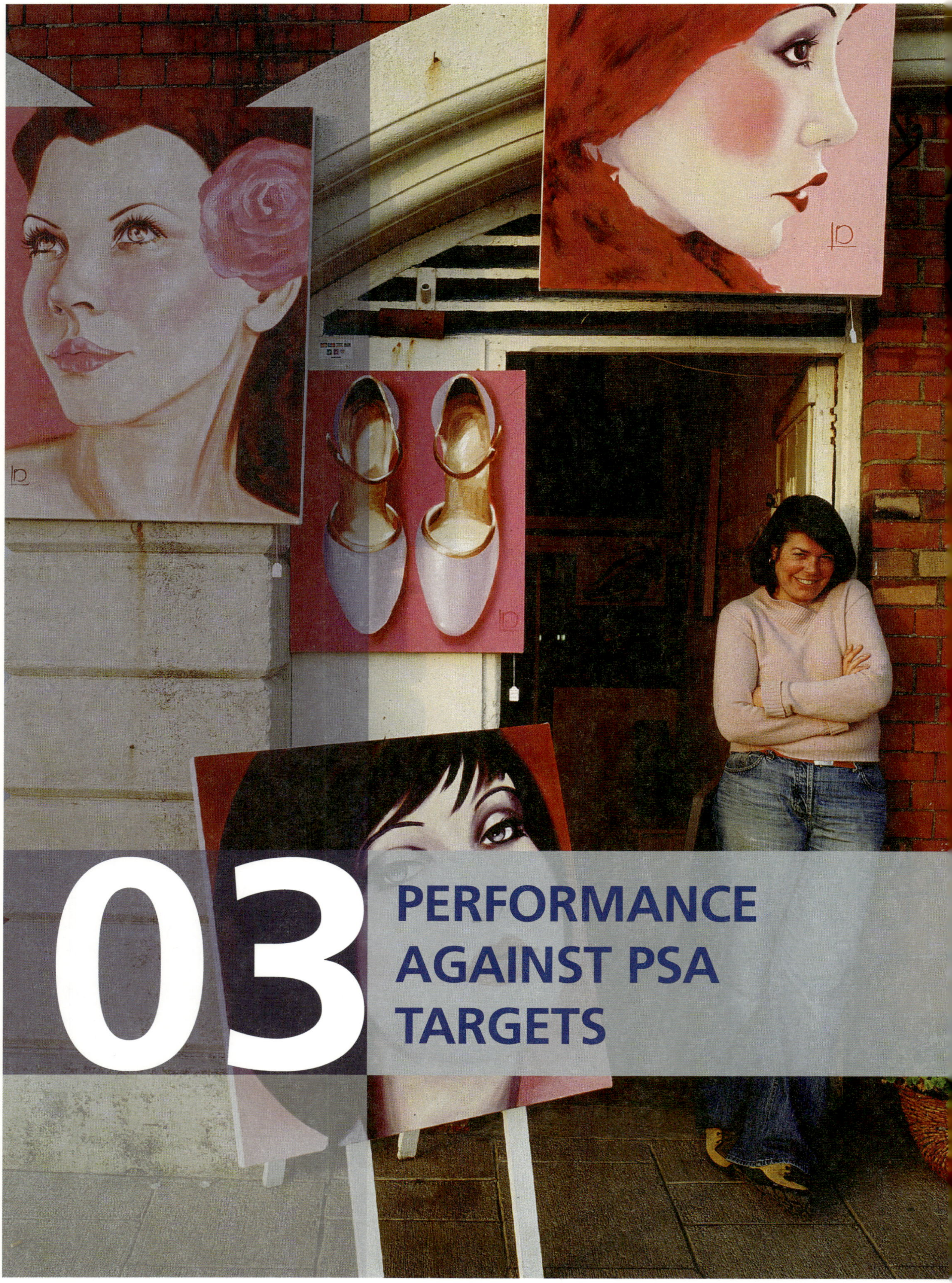

# 03 PERFORMANCE AGAINST PSA TARGETS

THIS CHAPTER GIVES AN ASSESSMENT OF PROGRESS AGAINST EACH OUTSTANDING PSA TARGET. IT IS STRUCTURED AROUND THE SR2004 TARGETS WHICH CAME INTO EFFECT IN APRIL 2005 AND IS SET OUT IN SIX PARTS:

- Part One – targets related to children (PSA 1, 2 and 3).
- Part Two – targets related to employment and safety in the workplace (PSA 4 and 5).
- Part Three – targets related to retirement (PSA 6 and 7).
- Part Four – target related to disabled people (PSA 8).
- Part Five – targets related to the quality of service (PSA 9 and 10).
- Part Six – efficiency and outstanding targets not rolled forward from previous Spending Reviews.

**21.** Where the SR2004 target takes forward an aim which was part of SR2002, an assessment of the latest position against the SR2002 target based on latest outturn data, is also provided. A summary table of all performance assessments is included at Figure 1.

### Measuring performance against targets

**22.** In order that judgements on final outturn against all PSA targets can be made on a consistent and comparable basis, the Department uses the terms set out below to describe performance.

### Ongoing targets

| Term | Usage |
| --- | --- |
| Met early | There is no possibility of subsequent slippage during the lifetime of the target. |
| Ahead | Progress is exceeding plans and expectations. |
| On course | Progress in line with plans and expectations. |
| Slippage | Progress is slower than expected, for example, by reference to criteria set out in a target's Technical Note. |
| Not yet assessed | New target for which data is not yet available. |

### Other targets

| Term | Usage |
| --- | --- |
| Met | Target achieved by the target date. |
| Met-ongoing | For older open-ended targets where the target level has been met and little would be achieved by continuing to report the same information indefinitely. |
| Partly met | Target has two or more distinct elements, and some – but not all – have been achieved by the target date. |
| Not met | Target was not met or met late. |

Figure 1 **Summary of performance towards all PSA targets**

| **SR2004 targets** | |
|---|---|
| **1a.** | Halve the number of children in relative low-income households between 1998–99 and 2010–11, on the way to eradicating child poverty by 2020 including – **current status: not yet assessed** |
| **1b.** | Reducing the proportion of children living in workless households by five per cent between spring 2005 and spring 2008 – **current status: not yet assessed** |
| **1c.** | Increasing the proportion of parents with care on Income Support and income-based Jobseeker's Allowance who receive maintenance for their children to 65 per cent by March 2008 – **current status: slippage** |
| Children in relative low income households element of target joint with HM Treasury. | |
| **2** | Improve children's communication, social and emotional development so that, by 2008, 50 per cent of children reach a good level of development at the end of the Foundation Stage and reduce inequalities between the level of development achieved by children in the 20 per cent most disadvantaged areas and the rest of England – **current status: not yet assessed** |
| Joint Target with Department for Education and Skills through the Sure Start Unit. | |
| **3.** | As a contribution to reducing the proportion of children living in households where no one is working, by 2008: |
| **3a.** | Increase the stock of Ofsted-registered childcare by ten per cent – **current status: met early** |
| **3b.** | Increase the take up of formal childcare by lower income working families by 50 per cent – **current status: not yet assessed** |
| **3c.** | Introduce, by April 2005, a successful light touch childcare approval scheme – **current status: on course** |
| Joint target with Department for Education and Skills through the Sure Start Unit. | |
| **4.** | As part of the wider objective of full employment in every region, over the three years to spring 2008, and taking account of the economic cycle: |
| **4a.** | Demonstrate progress on increasing the employment rate – **current status: on course** |
| Increase the employment rate of disadvantaged groups and significantly reduce the difference between the employment rates of the disadvantaged groups and the overall rate. | |
| **4b.** | Lone parents– **current status: not yet assessed** |
| **4c.** | Ethnic minorities – **current status: not yet assessed** |
| **4d.** | People aged 50 and over– **current status: not yet assessed** |

| | |
|---|---|
| **4e.** | Those with the lowest qualifications – **current status: on course** |
| **4f.** | Those living in the local authority wards with the poorest initial labour market position – **current status: not yet assessed** |
| Element 4a is joint target with HM Treasury. | |
| **5.** | By 2008 improve health and safety outcomes in Great Britain through progressive improvement in the control of risks from the workplace – **current status: not yet assessed** |
| **6.** | By 2008, be paying Pension Credit to at least 3.2 million pensioner households, while maintaining a focus on the most disadvantaged by ensuring that at least 2.2 million of these households are in receipt of the guarantee element – **current status: slippage** |
| **7.** | Improve working age individuals' awareness of their retirement provision such that by 2007-08: |
| **7a.** | 15.4 million individuals are regularly issued a pension forecast – **current status: on course** |
| **7b.** | 60,000 successful pension traces are undertaken a year – **current status: not yet assessed** |
| **8.** | In the three years to March 2008: |
| **8a.** | further improve the rights of disabled people and remove barriers to their participation in society, working with other government departments, including through increasing awareness of the rights of disabled people – **current status: slippage** |
| **8b and c.** | increase the employment rate of disabled people, and significantly reduce the difference between their employment rate and the overall rate, taking account of the economic cycle – **current status: not yet assessed** |
| **9.** | Improve Housing Benefit administration by: |
| **9a.** | reducing the average time taken to process a Housing Benefit claim to no more than 48 days nationally and across the bottom 15 per cent of local authorities to no more than 55 days, by March 2008 – **current status: on course** |
| **9b.** | increasing the number of cases in the deregulated private rented sector in receipt of Local Housing Allowance to 740,000 by 2008 – **current status: not yet assessed** |
| **9c.** | increasing the number of cases in receipt of the Local Housing Allowance where the rent is paid directly to the claimant to 470,000 by 2008 – **current status: not yet assessed** |

| | |
|---|---|
| **10.** | Reduce overpayments from fraud and error in: |
| **10a.** | Income Support and Jobseeker's Allowance – **current status: not yet assessed** |
| **10b.** | Housing Benefit – **current status: slippage** |

| SR2002 targets | |
|---|---|
| **1.** | Reduce the number of children in low-income households by at least a quarter by 2004, as a contribution towards the broader target of halving child poverty by 2010 and eradicating it by 2020 – **current status: not met – final assessment** |
| Joint target with HM Treasury. | |
| **2.** | Double the proportion of parents with care on Income Support and income-based Jobseeker's Allowance who receive maintenance for their children to 60 per cent by March 2006 – **current status: not met – final assessment** |
| **3.** | Demonstrate progress by spring 2006 on increasing the employment rate and reducing the unemployment rate over the economic cycle – **current status: on course** |
| Joint target with HM Treasury. | |
| **4.** | Over the three years to spring 2006, increase the employment rates of disadvantaged areas and groups, taking account of the economic cycle and significantly reduce the difference between their employment rates and the overall rate. |
| **4a.** | Lone parents – **current status: ahead** |
| **4b.** | Ethnic minorities – **current status: on course** |
| **4c.** | People aged 50 and over – **current status: on course** |
| **4d.** | Those with the lowest qualifications – **current status: on course** |
| **4e.** | Those living in the local authority wards with the poorest initial labour market position – **current status: on course** |
| Ethnic minorities element joint with Department of Trade and Industry. | |
| **5.** | Reduce the proportion of children in households with no one in work over the 3 years from spring 2003 to spring 2006 by 6.5 per cent – **current status: slippage** |
| **6.** | By 2006, be paying Pension Credit to at least 3 million pensioner households – **current status: not met – final assessment** |

| | |
|---|---|
| **7a.** | In the three years to 2006, increase the employment rate of people with disabilities, taking account of the economic cycle, and significantly reduce the difference between their employment rate and the overall rate – **current status: on course** |
| **7b.** | Work to improve the rights of disabled people and to remove barriers to their participation in society – **current status: met – final assessment** |
| **8.** | Make significant progress towards modernising welfare delivery so that by 2005, 85 per cent of customers have their benefit paid into their bank accounts. – **current status: met early – final assessment** |
| **9.** | Improve delivery of Department for Work and Pensions' services by setting published annual targets for each major business addressing accuracy, unit costs and customer service, becoming progressively more demanding over the three-year period. |
| **9a.** | The Pension Service – **current status: not yet assessed for 2005–06** |
| **9b.** | Child Support Agency – **current status: not yet assessed for 2005–06** |
| **9c.** | Jobcentre Plus – **current status: not yet assessed for 2005–06** |
| Disability and Carers Service[7] – **current status: not yet assessed for 2005–06** | |
| **10.** | Reduce losses from fraud and error for people of working age: |
| **10a.** | In Income Support and Jobseeker's Allowance, with a 33 per cent reduction by March 2004 and 50 per cent by 2006 – **current status: on course** |
| **10b.** | In Housing Benefit, with a 25 per cent reduction by 2006 – **current status: slippage** |

| **Outstanding Comprehensive Spending Review 1998 target** |
|---|
| Promote policies consistent with a change in the ratio of spending on pensions by the state to spending on pensions by the private sector from around 60:40 in 1998 to 50:50 by 2025 and to 40:60 in 50 years' time – **current assessment: ongoing** |

**7** Not part of PSA but included as additional information.

# PART ONE **CHILDREN**

## Objective: to ensure the best start for all children and end child poverty by 2020.

**SR2004 PSA target 1:** Halve the number of children in relative low-income households between 1998–99 and 2010–11, on the way to eradicating poverty by 2020, including:

- reducing the proportion of children living in workless households by 5 per cent between spring 2005 and spring 2008; and
- increasing the proportion of Parents with Care on Income Support and income-based Jobseeker's Allowance who receive maintenance for their children to 65 per cent by March 2008.

*Children in relative low-income households element joint with HM Treasury*

**PSA1a:** halve the number of children in relative low-income households between 1998-99 and 2010-11, on the way to eradicating poverty by 2020.

### Measurement

**23.** This target is monitored by reference to two separate measures:

- the number of children in households with income less than 60 per cent of contemporary median household income, compared with 1998–99; and
- the number of children in households with income less than 70 per cent of contemporary median household income, combined with material deprivation, compared with 1998–99.

**24.** The Government will also monitor progress against an absolute low income indicator. Absolute low-income households are defined as those with incomes below 60 per cent of median income held constant in real terms from a 1998–99 baseline.

### Children in households with less than 60 per cent of median income

**25.** Income is equivalised (adjusted to take into account variations in both the size and composition of the household) using the modified OECD equivalisation scale. This scale was chosen in order to ease international comparisons, and can only be used with income Before Housing Costs.

**The Government will also monitor progress against an absolute low income indicator.**

**26.** Progress will be measured on a United Kingdom, not a Great Britain basis. HBAI statistics on relative low-income have been able to cover the UK since 2002–03. Prior to this, the data was for GB only. This year, National Statistics have been able to estimate a UK baseline figure for 1998–99. Reporting on a UK basis increases the baseline for children living in households with less than 60 per cent of median income from 3.3 million to 3.4 million.

**27.** Between 1998–99 and 2004–05 the number of children living in households with less than 60 per cent of median income fell by 600,000.

### Children in households with less than 70 per cent of median income and in material deprivation

**28.** 2004–05 was the first year of data on material deprivation. The Government will set the baseline and threshold in 2006 for the target to halve by 2010–11 the number of children suffering a combination of material deprivation and who live in households with less than 70 per cent of median income by comparison with their number in 1998–99.

**29.** Additional background information on this target is available in the PSA Technical Note.[8]

### Performance

**30.** As the precise construction of the material deprivation indicator has not yet been determined, progress towards this target is **not yet assessed.**

**31. SR2002 target rolled forward:** PSA 1 – *reduce the number of children in low-income households by at least a quarter by 2004, as a contribution towards the broader target of halving child poverty by 2010 and eradicating it by 2020.*

### SR2002 Measurement

**32.** Information on this target is available in the PSA Technical Note.[9]

### SR2002 Performance

**33.** This target was **not met** – final assessment.

**34.** Between 1998–99 and 2004–05 the number of children living in relative low-income households fell:

- by 700,000 from 3.1 million to 2.4 million on a before housing costs (BHC) basis; and

- by 700,000 from 4.1 million to 3.4 million on an after housing costs (AHC) basis.

**35.** While encouraging, the progress since 1998-99 was not quite enough to meet the PSA target to reduce the number of children living in relative low income by a quarter. The percentage reduction in this period was 23 per cent BHC and 17 per cent AHC. The PSA target has been narrowly missed on a BHC basis by 100,000 and missed on an AHC basis by 300,000 children.

**8** www.dwp.gov.uk/publications/dwp/2004/psa/tech_note_2005_2008.pdf

**9** www.dwp.gov.uk/publications/dwp/2002/sda/oct/tn_oct.asp

Figure 2 **Children living in relative low-income households (SR2002 target)**

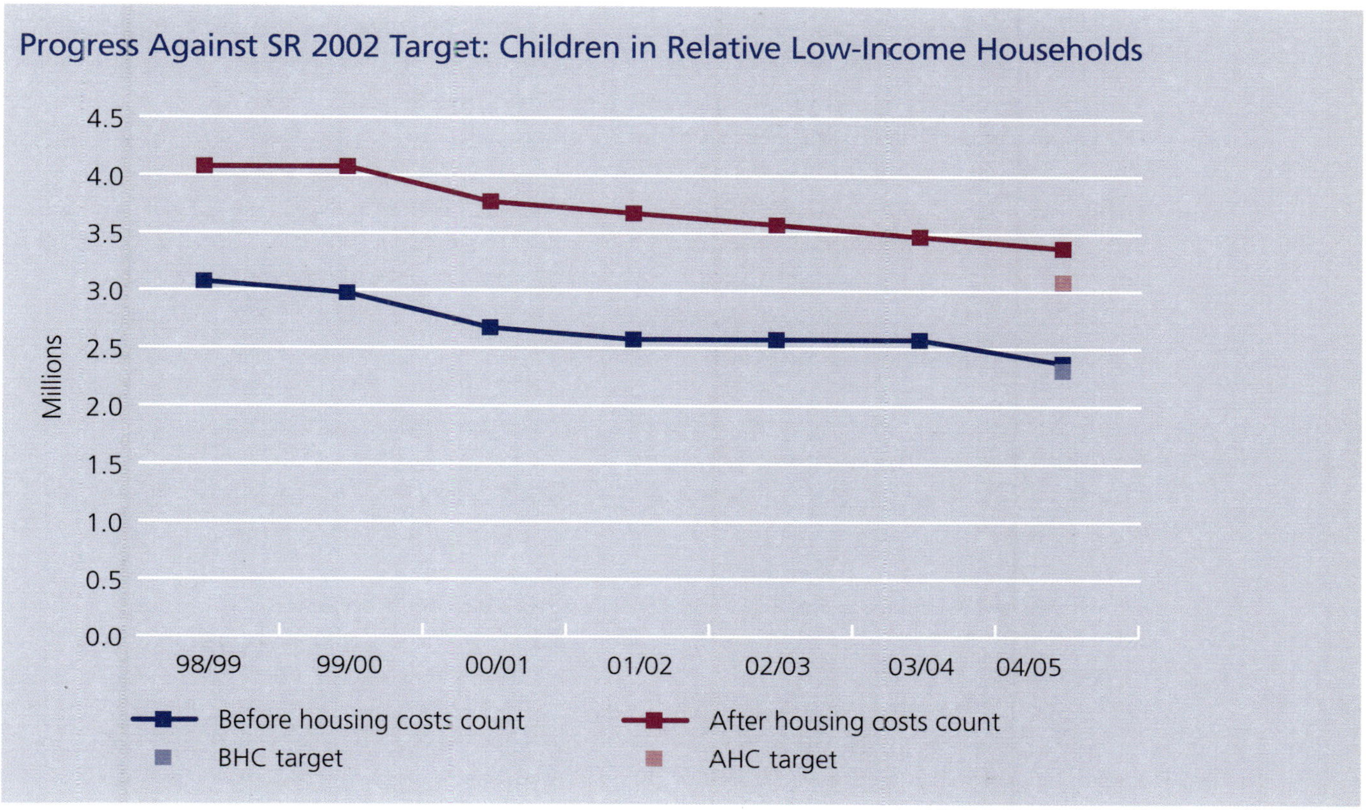


## Reasons for progress

**36.** The Government set itself an extremely challenging target against which substantial progress has been made.

**37.** Despite the SR2002 target not having been met, significant inroads have been made into reducing the number of children in relative low-income households, which shows that the strategy of financial support for families combined with continued progress against employment targets has been successful.

- As a result of the Government's reforms to the tax and benefit system since 1997, by October 2006, in real terms:
  - families with children will be, on average, £1,500 a year better off, while those in the poorest fifth will be, on average, £3,400 per year better off;
  - a single-earner family on half average male earnings with two children will be £3,950 better off; and
  - a single-earner family on average male earnings with two young children will be £235 a year better off.

- The number of children in workless households in GB has fallen by 370,000 since autumn 1997.
- The lone parent employment rate has increased from 45.3 per cent in spring 1997 to 56.6 per cent in spring 2005.

**38.** The Government remains firmly committed to the challenging goals to halve and then eradicate child poverty, and will continue to increase the financial support available to families with children, make further progress on its employment strategies, and improve public services.

**PSA 1b: reduce the proportion of children living in workless households by 5 per cent between spring 2005 and spring 2008.**

### Measurement

**39.** The baseline for this target is the proportion of children in workless households at spring (March–May) 2005 – 15.7 per cent.[10] Progress is monitored every six months on the basis of both spring and autumn data.

**40.** Further information on this target is available in the PSA Technical Note.[11]

### Performance

**41.** Performance against the spring 2005 baseline is **not yet assessed**. The spring 2006 figures, available in July 2006, will provide the first indication of progress against the target. Figure 3 shows progress to date and the required future trajectory to meet PSA 1b by spring 2008.

**42. SR2002 target rolled forward:**
PSA 5 – *reduce the proportion of children in households with no one in work over the three years from spring 2003 to spring 2006 by 6.5 per cent.*

**The Government remains firmly committed to the challenging goals to halve and then eradicate child poverty.**

**10** Source: Household Labour Force Survey.
**11** www.dwp.gov.uk/publications/dwp/2004/psa/tech_note_2005_2008.pdf

Figure 3 **Proportion of children living in workless households – 2008 trajectory**

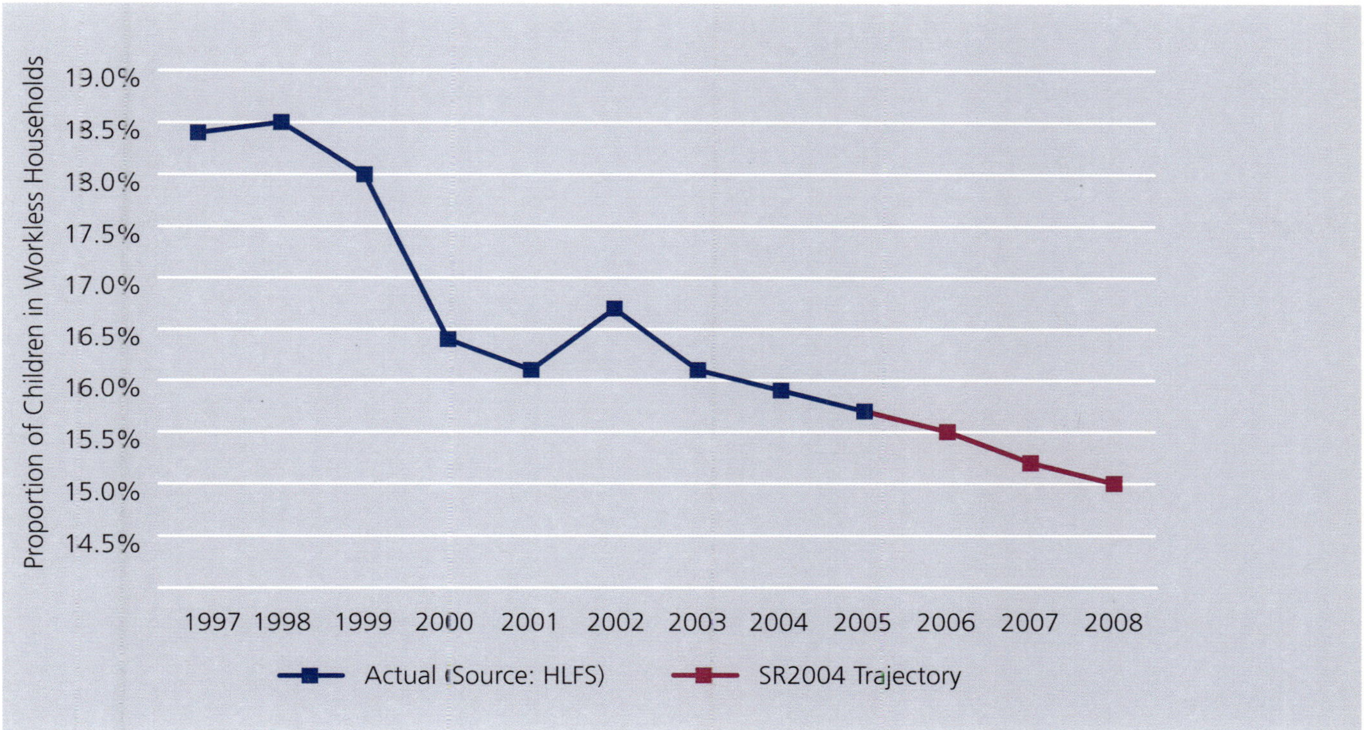


## SR2002 Performance

**43.** There has been some **slippage** in progress towards this target.

**44.** A 6.5 per cent reduction means that by spring 2006, only 15.1 per cent of children should be living in workless households. Data for spring 2006 will be available in July 2006.

**45.** The latest information available is for autumn 2005, when the proportion of children living in workless households was 15.9 per cent, an increase of 0.9 percentage points on autumn 2004, but a fall of 2.6 percentage points on the autumn 1997 figure. As data is not seasonally adjusted, comparisons can only be made year on year and these figures are therefore not directly comparable to the spring data used in the measurement of this target. However, they suggest that the likelihood of achieving the SR2002 target is small.

Figure 4 **Proportion of children living in workless households – 2006 trajectory**

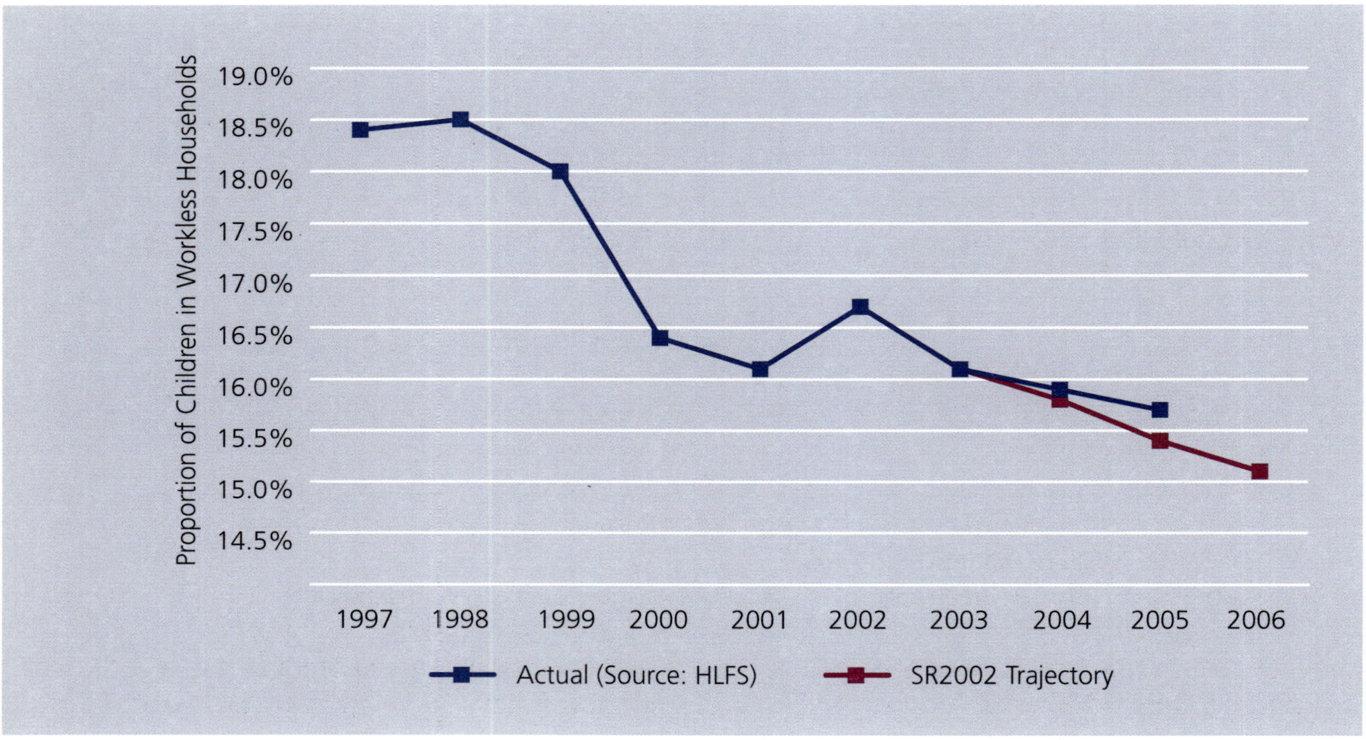


## Improving performance

**46.** Given the resources available to it, the Department's strategy is to support and consolidate the existing lone parent strategy. This is because:

- two thirds of children in workless households live in households that contain a lone parent; and
- policies on partners are not expected to deliver significant outcomes in the short term.

More information about the lone parent strategy can be found under PSA 4b.

**PSA1c: increase the proportion of parents with care on Income Support and income-based Jobseeker's Allowance who receive maintenance for their children to 65 per cent by March 2008.**

## Measurement

**47.** Performance against the target will be measured using data from the Department's Child Support and Income Support computer systems, and includes applications administered under both the old and new child support schemes, which have had a maintenance calculation or assessment performed, including those for which the liability resulted in a nil amount.

**48.** As this target is rolled forward from SR2002, the baseline remains October 2002 when the proportion of parents with care on benefit receiving maintenance was estimated at around 30 per cent.

**49.** Full details of the data sources used and background information to this target are available in the PSA Technical Note.[12]

**50.** The figures provided are interim estimates based on the best information currently available and, as such, may be subject to change in the future.

**51.** Although the target is defined in terms of parents/persons with care in receipt of benefit or those who are the partner of a benefit recipient, the Department is unable to report on partners of benefit recipients due to data limitations resulting from problems with the new IT system. Work is continuing to resolve these problems.

### Performance

**52.** There is **slippage** in progress towards this target. Latest data available (November 2005) shows that 25 per cent of parents with care on benefit are now in receipt of maintenance.

**53.** Achievement of the target is dependent upon the successful conversion of old scheme cases onto the new scheme, by December 2007. The review carried out by the CSA Chief Executive in 2005 demonstrated how difficult and resource-intensive conversion would be. The Department is keeping this under review and has asked Sir David Henshaw to address it in his redesign of Child Support, commissioned by the Secretary of State in February 2006.[13]

### Improving performance

**54.** The Agency's Operational Improvement Plan published in February 2006[14] aims to bring about:

- changes to the Agency's structure and streamlining of processes which will enable significant improvements in productivity, reduction in backlogs and faster clearance of applications;
- more effective collection and payment;
- a substantial increase in numbers of staff dedicated to enforcing liabilities, increased levels of compliance and debt recovery;
- restructuring to increase focus on the lifecycle of cases, senior caseworkers to resolve more complex cases and more staff deployed to deal directly with clients.

**55.** The Agency has published a new package of targets for 2006-07, which are designed to reflect Ministerial and Agency priorities and to focus the Agency's efforts on delivery of the Operational Improvement Plan.

## The Department's strategy is to support and consolidate the existing lone parent strategy.

12 www.dwp.gov.uk/publications/dwp/2004/psa/tech_note_2005_2008.pdf
13 www.csa.gov.uk/pdf/english/reports/redesigntor.pdf
14 www.csa.gov.uk/pdf/english/reports/oip.pdf

Figure 5 **Proportion of parents with care on Income Support/Jobseeker's Allowance in receipt of maintenance**

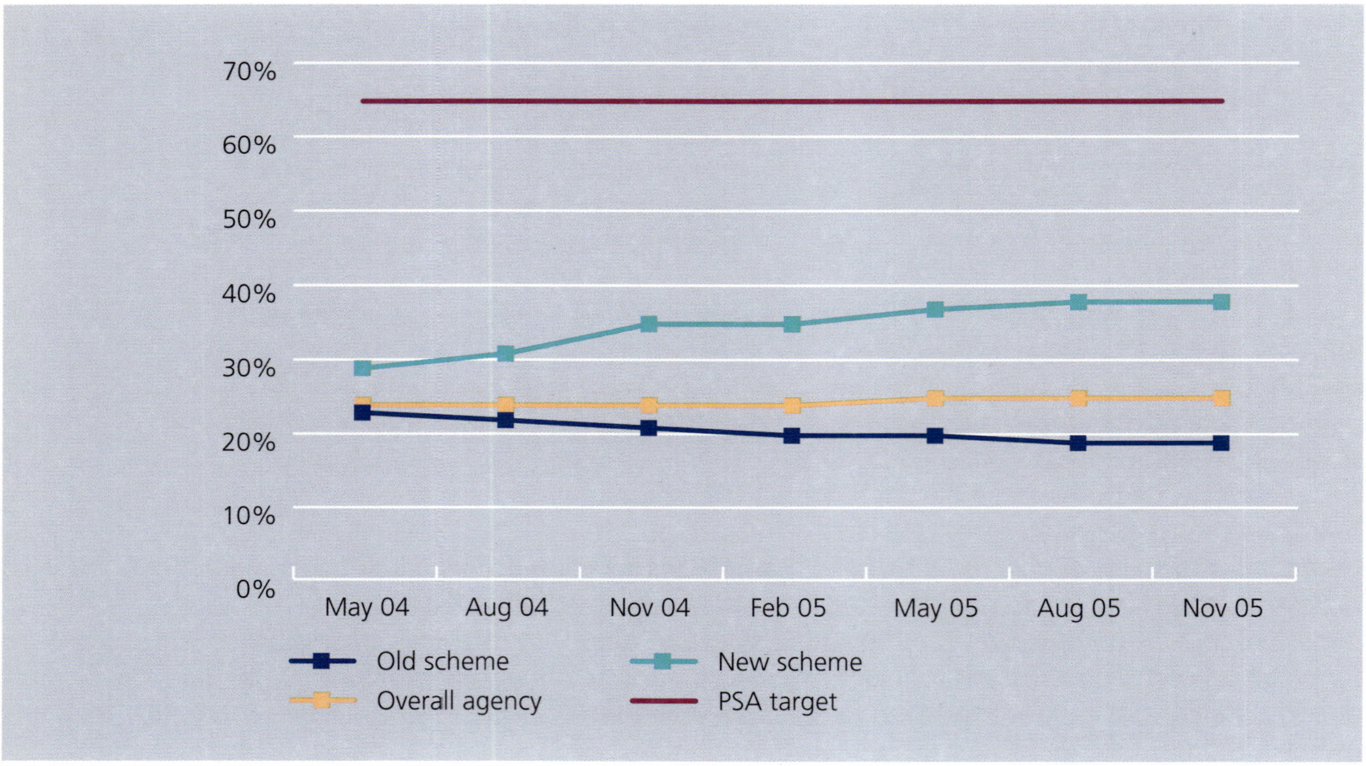


**56.** SR2002 target rolled forward:
PSA 2 – *double the proportion of parents with care on Income Support and income-based Jobseeker's Allowance who receive maintenance for their children to 60 per cent by March 2006.*

**SR2002 Performance**

**57.** This target was **not met**. Achievement of this target was critically dependent on the conversion of old scheme cases onto the new scheme. Completion of conversion by March 2006 has not proved possible.

**SR2004 PSA target 2:** Improve children's communication, social and emotional development so that by 2008, 53 per cent of children reach a good level of development at the end of the Foundation Stage and reduce inequalities between the level of development achieved by children in the 20 per cent most disadvantaged areas and the rest of England.

*Joint target with Department for Education and Skills and only relates to England, as provision of early years services and childcare are devolved issues.*

## Measurement

**58.** This target will be measured against the 2005 baseline and will identify how many children have reached a good level[15] of personal, social and emotional development and a good level of communication, language and literacy at the end of the Foundation Stage. Measurement is based on the Foundation Stage Profile which is owned by the Qualifications and Curriculum Agency. The school year in which most children reach the age of 5 is the relevant data period and refers to all children completing the Foundation Stage in that particular year. Further information on this target is available in the PSA Technical Note.[16]

**59.** The original 50 per cent level was provisional and has been revised to 53 per cent, reflecting the Government's ambition for improving children's development. A target for reducing inequalities in achievement between children in deprived areas and those in the rest of England has been set at 4 per cent. The reduction in inequalities will be assessed by comparing the performance of children living in the 30 per cent most deprived Super Output Areas (equivalent to the 20 per cent most disadvantaged wards) with the national average.

## Performance

**60.** Performance against this target is **not yet assessed**. The 2005 baseline is that 48 per cent of children reached a good level of development at the end of the Foundation Stage. The gap between those reaching this level in disadvantaged areas and the rest of England was 16 per cent.

## Reasons for progress

- In its most recent quality report, *Early Years: Firm Foundations* published in August 2005[17] and based on evidence from inspections carried out over the last two years, Ofsted confirmed that 92 per cent of Government-funded free early education delivered by private and voluntary providers is of high quality.

- The Department for Education and Skills' Primary National Strategy with a team of regional advisers providing support to local authorities in delivering effective early years practice, which should raise the proportion of children reaching good levels of development.

15 A score of six points on all seven assessment scales.
16 www.dwp.gov.uk/publications/dwp/2004/psa/tech_note_2005_2008.pdf

17 www.ofsted.gov.uk/publications/firmfoundations/preface.htm

**SR2004 PSA target 3:** As a contribution to reducing the proportion of children living in households where no one is working, by 2008:

- increase the stock of Ofsted-registered childcare by 10 per cent;
- increase the take up of formal childcare by lower-income working families by 50 per cent; and
- introduce, by April 2005, a successful light-touch childcare approval scheme.

*Joint target with Department for Education and Skills and only relates to England, as provision of early years services and childcare are devolved issues.*

**PSA 3a:** increase the stock of Ofsted-registered childcare by 10 per cent

### Measurement

**61.** Progress is measured against a March 2004 baseline of 1,103,000 Ofsted-registered childcare places in England. The aim is to increase the stock of childcare by 10 per cent, which represents a target of 1,213,000 registered places. Measurement is based on Ofsted's quarterly childcare places registration data. Ofsted-registered childcare covers an estimated 92 per cent of total childcare places. Further detail on this target is available from the PSA Technical Note.[18]

Figure 6 **Ofsted-registered childcare places in England**

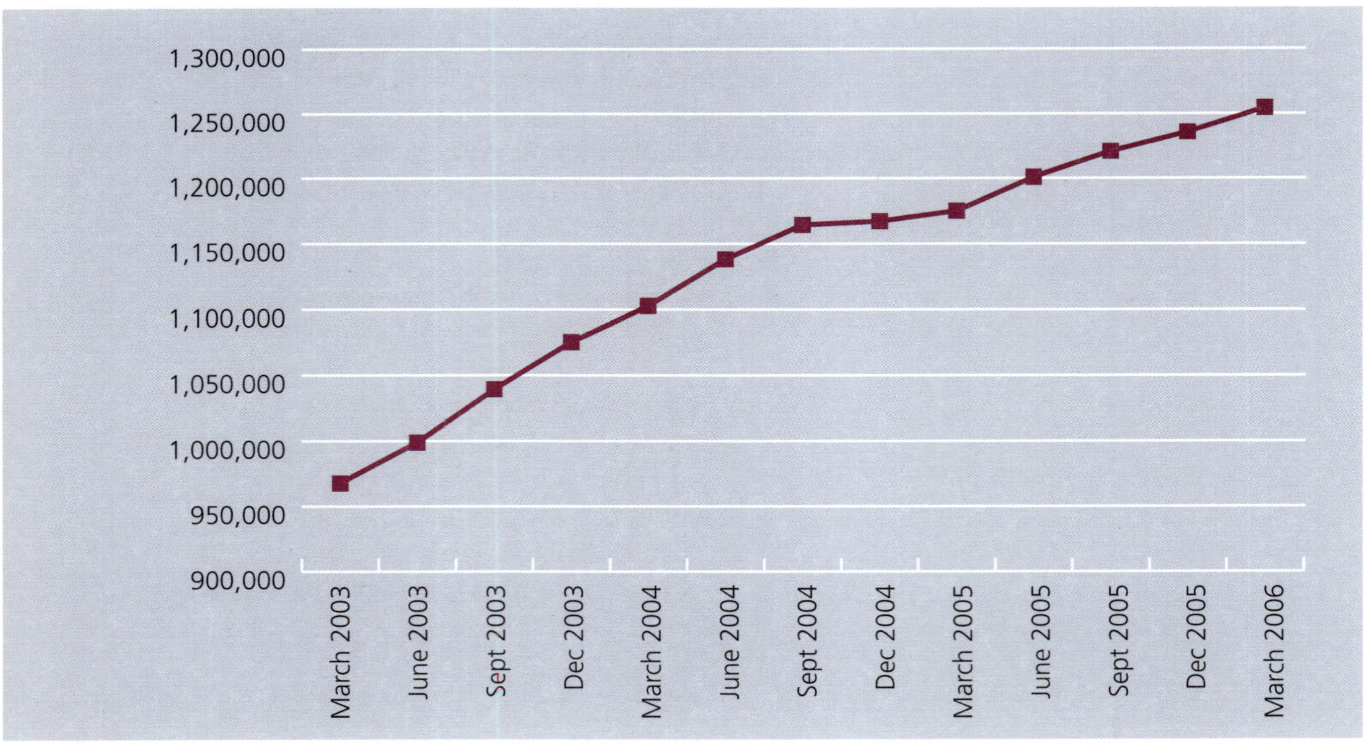


18 www.dwp.gov.uk/publications/dwp/2004/psa/tech_note_2005_2008.pdf

### Performance

**62.** This target has been **met early**. In September 2005 the stock of childcare places stood at 1,221,000, exceeding the required target. This rose further to over 1,250,000 places in March 2006, an increase of more than 13 per cent from the March 2004 baseline.

## PSA 3b: increase the take up of formal childcare by lower-income working families by 50 per cent

### Measurement

**63.** The baseline for measuring this target has not been assessed and the 50 per cent target is provisional. The baseline and target will be confirmed later in the year.

### Performance

**64.** Performance against this target is **not yet assessed**. However, there has been a 13 per cent growth in registered childcare over the two years from March 2004, with particularly strong growth in full day care and out-of-school provision which should help facilitate the take-up of formal childcare by lower-income working families. Department for Work and Pensions administrative data on children in workless households shows faster progress in Sure Start areas than other areas and HM Revenue and Customs data on take-up of the childcare element in Working Tax Credits also shows an approximate five per cent increase between April 2004 and April 2005.

### Reasons for progress

- Facilitation of the childcare market by local authorities, using General Sure Start Grant funding, has helped to address unmet needs for childcare, particularly for lower-income families.

- Better integrated and focused services in disadvantaged areas resulting from the rollout of the Ten-year Childcare Strategy, have helped to improve access for lower-income families.

- Entitlement to a free pre-school place for 3- and 4-year-olds.
- The central role of Jobcentre Plus in promoting the benefits of formal childcare to parents at the point of transition into work.

**There has been a 12 per cent growth in registered childcare over the two years from March 2004.**

**PSA 3c: introduce, by April 2005, a successful light-touch childcare approval scheme**

### Measurement

**65.** Introduction of the Childcare Approval Scheme will be judged successful if:

- milestones are reached as per the agreed timetable;[19]
- the scheme has the ability to provide an efficient service with an 80 per cent turnaround time of six weeks;
- the standard of service is achieved at a fee for individuals not higher than £125 per approval; and
- 15,000 approvals are achieved[20] during the year ending 31 March 2008.

Further detail on this target is available from the PSA Technical Note.

### Performance

**66.** This sub-target is **on course**. The Childcare Approval Scheme was established with the necessary cost and quality provisions in place in April 2005. The PSA Technical Note requires that the 15,000 indicator should be reviewed at the end of the first year of the scheme. This figure has been revised to 3,500 approvals in total by spring 2008. At 31 March 2006, a total of 1,715 carers had been approved.

**19** See PSA Technical Note at: www.dwp.gov.uk/publications/dwp/2004/psa/tech_note_2005_2008.pdf

**20** The 2008 level of approvals will be confirmed following receipt of data on take-up of measures on employer-supported childcare and on the number of approvals achieved by the end of the first year of the light touch approval scheme in April 2006.

# PART TWO **EMPLOYMENT AND WELL-BEING AT WORK**

**Objective: to promote work as the best form of welfare for people of working age, while protecting the position of those in greatest need.**

**SR2004 PSA target 4:** As part of the wider objective of full employment in every region, over the three years to spring 2008, and taking account of the economic cycle:

- demonstrate progress on increasing the employment rate;
- increase the employment rates of disadvantaged groups (lone parents, ethnic minorities, people aged 50 and over, those with the lowest qualifications and those living in local authority wards with the poorest initial labour market position); and
- significantly reduce the difference between the employment rates of the disadvantaged groups and the overall rate.

*The overall employment rate element is joint with HM Treasury.*

**PSA 4a:** demonstrate progress on increasing the employment rate (joint target with HM Treasury).

### Measurement

**67.** The baseline against which this target is measured is spring 2005, when the GB employment rate was 74.9 per cent. The target is monitored using seasonally adjusted Labour Force Survey (LFS) quarterly data.[21] Structural improvements in the employment rate are determined by controlling for the impact of wider economic developments.[22] Additional information on this target is available in the PSA Technical Note.[23]

### Performance

**68.** Progress towards this target is **on course**. The employment rate is available on a rolling quarterly basis, and latest data shows the GB rate at 74.6 per cent (December-February 2006). This is lower than the baseline of 74.9 per cent, but follows a year in which economic growth has been considerably weaker than in previous years. The fact that the employment rate has remained steady in the face of this is an encouraging sign that the labour market remains strong. Figure 7 overleaf shows the long-term trend in the employment rate.

**69. SR2002 target rolled forward:**
PSA 3 – *demonstrate progress by spring 2006 on increasing the employment rate and reducing the unemployment rate over the economic cycle [Joint target with HM Treasury].*

**21** This has a sampling variability of 0.3 percentage points.
**22** Information on the economic cycle is published by HM Treasury in Pre-Budget Reports and Financial Statement and Budget Reports. More detail can be found in the PSA Technical Note.
**23** www.dwp.gov.uk/publications/dwp/2004/psa/tech_note_2005_2008.pdf

## SR2002 Performance

**70.** The Department is **on course** to meet both the employment and unemployment components of this target.

**71.** Latest figures show that for the December-February 2006 quarter, UK and GB employment rates stood at 74.5 and 74.6 per cent respectively. The UK employment rate remains one of the highest of the G7 group of industrialised countries. The economy is currently growing below trend, and at the start of the current economic cycle (H1 1997) – which is an on-trend point – the employment rate was 72.9 per cent.

**72.** At 5.2 per cent (December–February 2006), the UK has the third lowest ILO unemployment rate of the G7 group of industrialised countries (after Japan and the USA). The GB unemployment rate as at December–February 2006 was 5.2 per cent, compared to 5.0 per cent at the start of the SR02 period (spring 2003) and 7.2 per cent at the start of the current economic cycle (spring 1997). So the unemployment rate has risen slightly since the start of the SR02 period, but it is lower than at the start of the current economic cycle, which is an on-trend point.

**73.** Since the economy is currently estimated to be below trend, and since it is reasonable to expect that on returning to trend, the labour market will strengthen further, it is clear that there is a significant structural improvement in both the unemployment rate and the employment rate over the current economic cycle.

Figure 7 **GB employment rate**

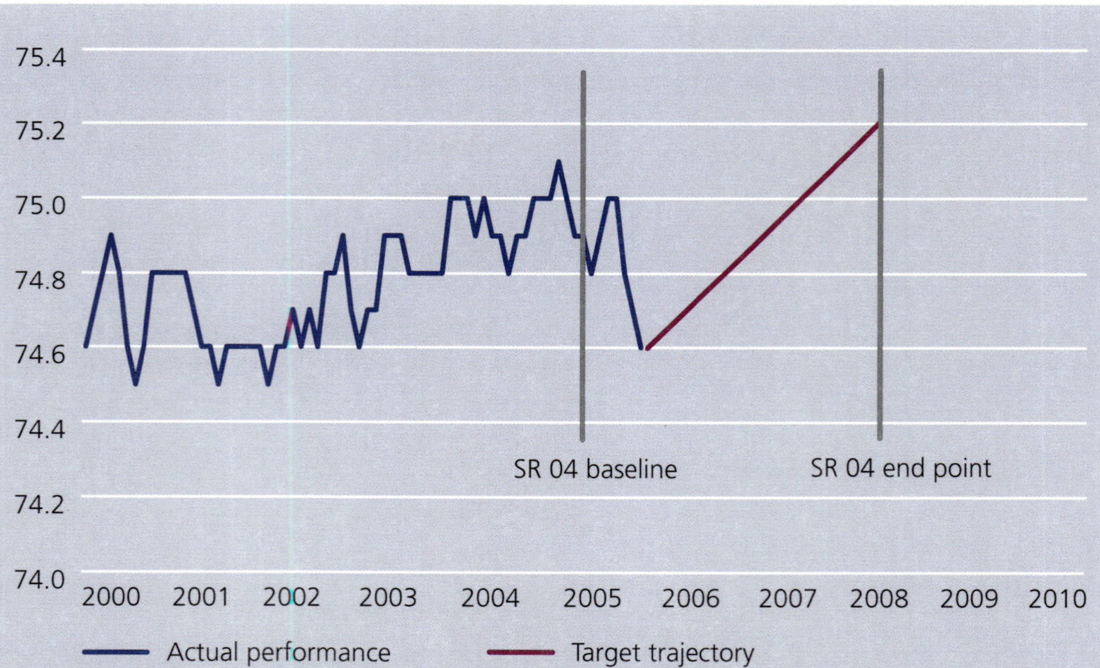


Note: The SR04 baseline is 74.9 per cent, in spring 2005. The target trajectory is based on increasing the employment rate from the latest available value (74.6 per cent for December–February 2006) to a value 0.3 percentage points higher than the baseline value (75.2 per cent). This is because 0.3 percentage points is the confidence interval of the employment rate measurement, so an increase of 0.3 points or more can be deemed to be statistically significant. This analysis ignores any adjustments made for changes in the economic cycle, which cannot be forecast at this time.

### Reasons for progress

**74.** The Department continues to implement its active labour market policies, aimed at reducing the number of people out of work. These include:

- tackling unemployment through the Jobseeker's Allowance regime, as delivered through the Jobcentre Plus network;
- tackling inactivity through a more work-focused welfare delivery system, such as the Pathways to Work pilot for people on incapacity benefit, New Deal for Lone Parents and New Deal for Disabled People;
- working with the private sector through New Deal options and Employment Zones; and
- increasing labour supply through making work pay – the minimum wage and working tax credits are examples.

**75.** It is the success of these policies, combined with a largely stable macro-economy, which have resulted in the continued strength of the GB labour market.

**PSA 4b: increase the employment rate of lone parents and significantly reduce the difference between the employment rate of this group and the overall rate.**

### Measurement

**76.** The baseline for this target is the spring 2005 lone parent employment rate of 56.6 per cent, and the gap with the overall rate of 18 percentage points. Data is obtained from the Household LFS.

**77.** A significant increase in the lone parent employment rate is defined in the Technical Note[24] as at least a two percentage point increase in the Spending Review period. Similarly, the gap with the overall rate has to close by at least two percentage points for the reduction to be significant.

### Performance

**78.** Performance against the spring 2005 baseline is **not yet assessed**, because spring 2006 data will not be available until July 2006. The good performance of the lone parent employment rate to spring 2005 has made this target slightly more challenging.

**79. SR2002 target rolled forward:**
PSA 4a – *over the three years to spring 2006, increase the employment rate of lone parents, taking account of the economic cycle and significantly reduce the difference between their employment rate and the overall rate.*

**24** www.dwp.gov.uk/publications/dwp/2004/psa/tech_note_2005_2008.pdf

Figure 8 **Employment rates of lone parents, GB (overall) and SR04 target**

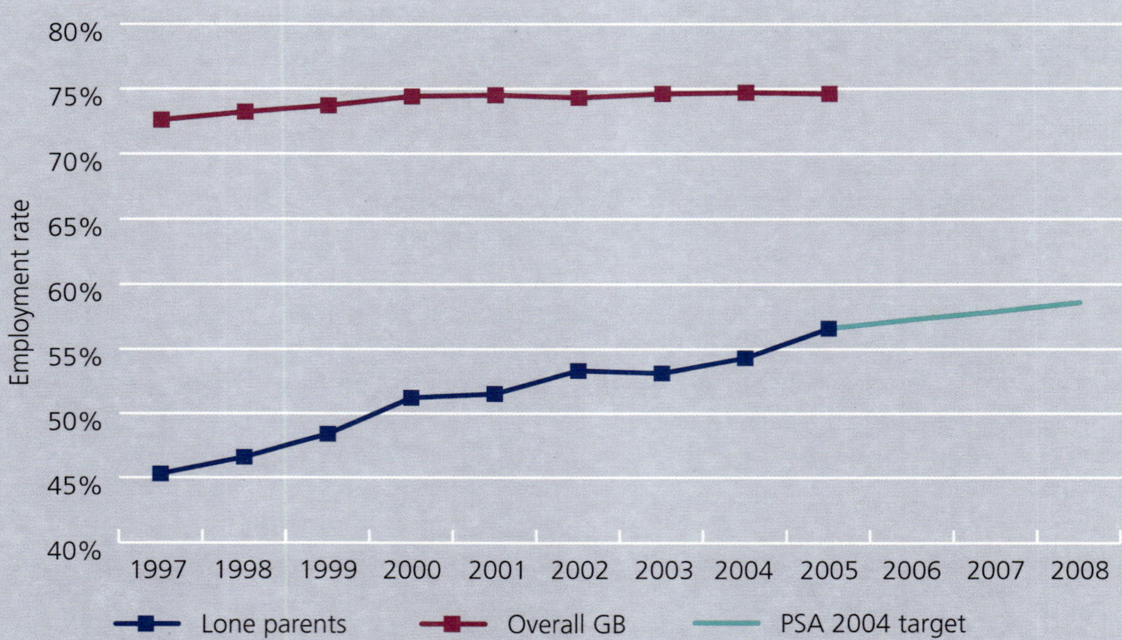


Source: Household Labour Force Survey, spring 2005

### SR2002 Performance

**80.** Progress towards the March 2006 milestone is **ahead** of expectations. The baseline for this target is the spring 2003 lone parent employment rate of 53.1 per cent, and the gap with the overall rate of 21.5 percentage points. At spring 2005 the employment rate was 56.6 per cent which represents a rise of 2.3 percentage points on the year.

### Reasons for progress

**81.** The increase in the lone parent employment rate in spring 2005 put the Department on course to meet the SR2002 target. The required increase of two percentage points from the baseline means that by spring 2006, the lone parent employment rate should be at least 55.1 per cent. Given that this has already been achieved, the SR2002 target will be met provided the rate does not decline by more than 1.5 percentage points over the remainder of the 2002 Spending Review period.

Figure 9 **Employment rates of lone parents, GB (overall) and the SR02 target**

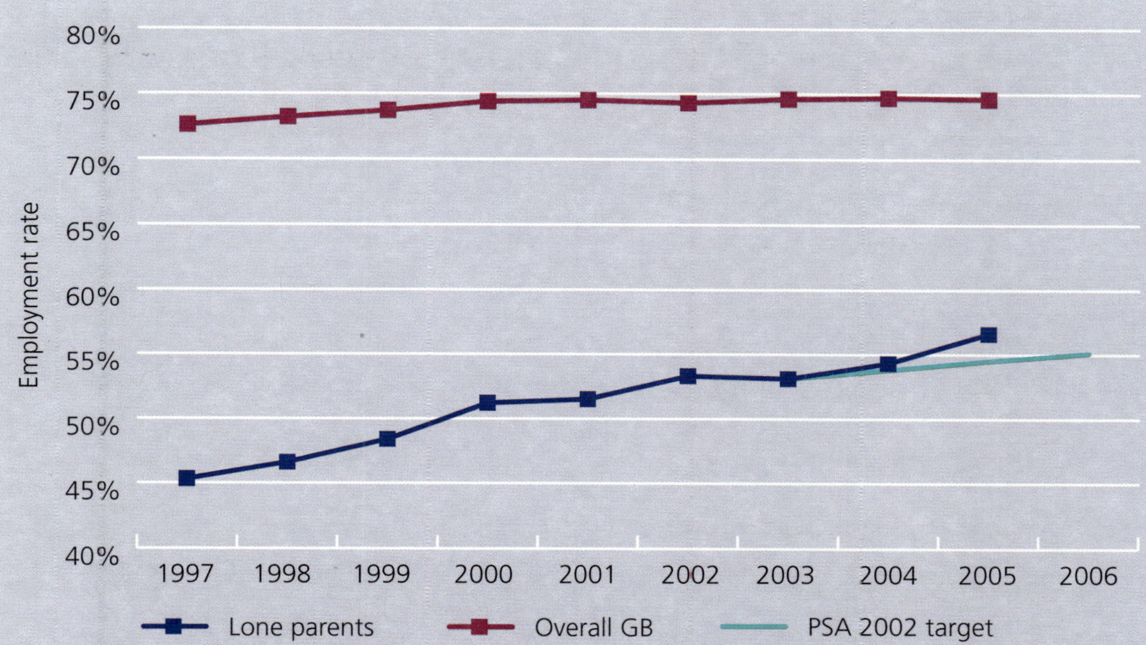


Source: Household Labour Force Survey, spring 2005

**82.** The main actions contributing to the reported level of performance include:

- increasing work focus – mandatory work-focused interviews and participation in the voluntary New Deal for Lone Parents provide the help and support needed to enter the labour market;

- financial incentives – measures such as the National Minimum Wage and Tax Credits have eased the immediate transition into work as well as providing more long-term support to make work pay; and

- childcare – the continued implementation of the National Childcare Strategy has increased access to childcare places.

**The Department continues to implement its active labour market policies, aimed at reducing the number of people out of work.**

**PSA 4c: increase the employment rate of ethnic minorities and significantly reduce the difference between the employment rate of this group and the overall rate.**

### Measurement

**83.** The baseline ethnic minority employment rate is spring (March–May) 2005, which was 58.4 per cent. The baseline figure for the gap between this ethnic minority employment rate and the overall employment rate for Great Britain is 16.2 percentage points.

**84.** A significant increase in the ethnic minority employment rate is defined in the PSA Technical Note[25] as at least a one percentage point increase in the Spending Review period. Similarly, the gap with the overall rate has to close by at least one percentage point for the reduction to be significant.

**85.** The ethnic minority employment rate is based on aggregated data for all respondents to the Labour Force Survey who classify themselves as belonging to a non-white ethnic group. The Labour Force Survey is also used to measure progress.

### Performance

**86.** Performance is **not yet assessed**. Only two quarters of data are currently available.

**87. SR2002 target rolled forward – PSA 4b:** *Over the three years to spring 2006, increase the employment rate of ethnic minorities and significantly reduce the difference between the employment rate of this group and the overall rate [Joint target with Department of Trade and Industry].*

### SR2002 Performance

**88.** The Department is currently **on course** to meet this target. At the spring 2003 baseline, the ethnic minority employment rate stood at 57.8 per cent with an employment rate gap of 16.9 percentage points. Latest performance estimates show an ethnic minority employment rate of 59.1 per cent and a gap against the overall rate of 15.7 percentage points.

**89.** The overall GB employment rate has structurally improved (see PSA4a). As the ethnic minority employment rate has increased by 1.3 percentage points, with the gap against the overall population narrowing by 1.2 percentage points from the 2003 baseline, this implies the ethnic minority employment rate has structurally improved over the economic cycle. The ethnic minority employment rate was 54.8 per cent in spring 1997, at the start of the economic cycle; this is over 5 percentage points lower than latest estimates and shows a significant improvement over the economic cycle.

**25** www.dwp.gov.uk/publications/dwp/2004/psa/tech_note_2005_2008.pdf

Figure 10 **Ethnic minority employment rate and gap with overall GB rate**

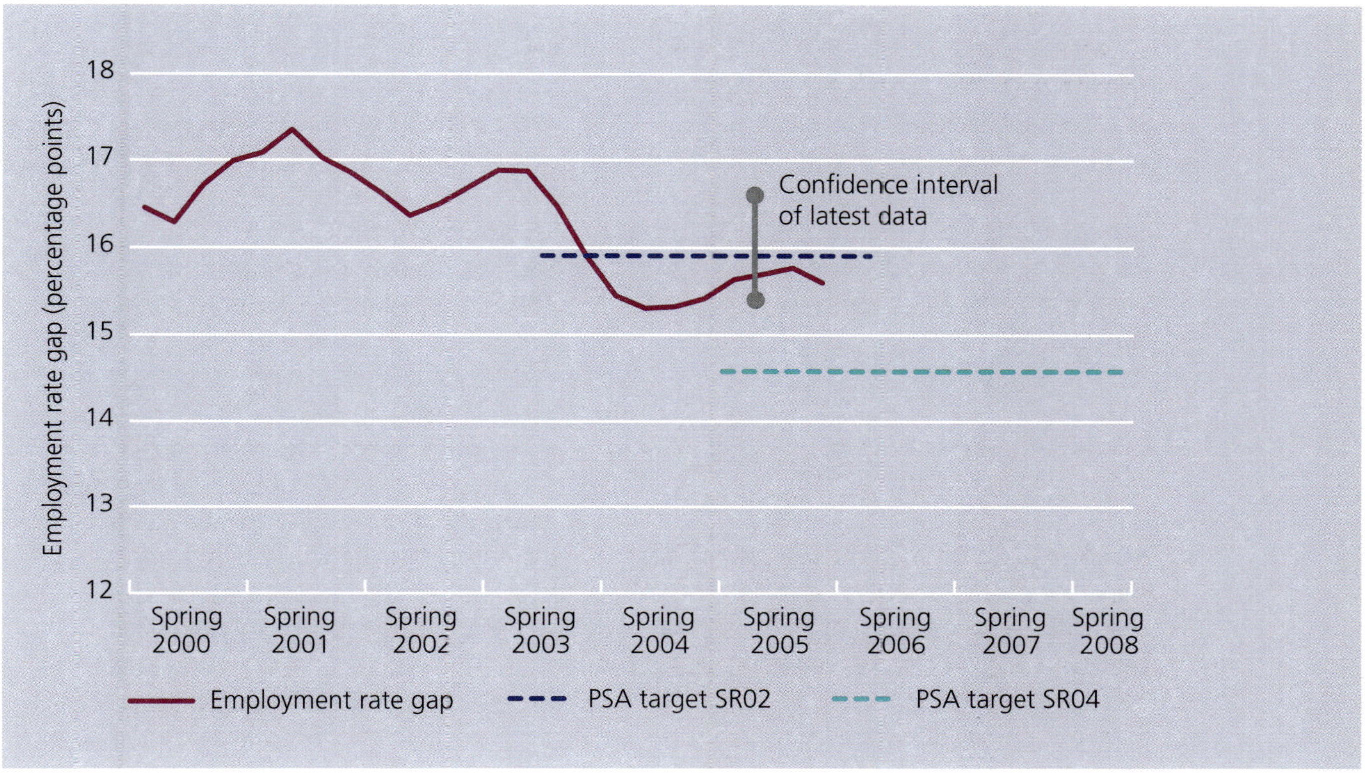


## Reasons for progress

**90.** This target forms part of the Government-wide Community Cohesion and Race Equality strategy.

**91.** There are three main barriers to employment faced by people from ethnic minority communities – lack of human capital, living in deprived areas and the 'ethnic penalty', of which employer discrimination is a significant part. A cross-government strategy, which is overseen by the Ethnic Minority Employment Task Force, aims to tackle these barriers and raise the ethnic minority employment rate.

**92.** The Departmental strategy to meet the target includes:

- ensuring that Jobcentre Plus has the ability to provide best-value programmes for ethnic minority clients;
- focusing resource and effort in areas of high unemployment and higher numbers of ethnic minorities;
- creating more flexibility to allow managers to develop local responses to the needs of ethnic minority groups;
- testing new ways of using public procurement to promote race equality; and

- finding new ways to reach people who, for one reason or another, are not in touch with current employment help.

**93.** Full details of the various programmes and initiatives which are in place to implement the cross-government strategy can be found in the annual report of the Ethnic Minority Employment Task Force.[26]

**PSA 4d: increase the employment rate of people aged 50 and over and significantly reduce the difference between the employment rate of this group and the overall rate.**

### Measurement

**94.** The baseline is spring (March–May) 2005 when the employment rate for the age 50 to 69 group was 54.7 per cent, 19.9 percentage points lower than the overall rate. The employment rate is based on ILO definitions, using estimates from the Labour Force Survey. Data is received quarterly and is not seasonally adjusted.

**95.** This target now looks at the employment of 50 to 69-year-olds, to reflect the fact that around one million people over state pension age are currently in work. The Government now has a range of policies to support those over state pension age who want to work.

### Performance

**96.** Progress on this target is **not yet assessed**. Only a relatively short run of data is available after the baseline. The estimated employment rate of those aged 50 to 69 in autumn 2005 was 54.8 per cent, 19.9 percentage points lower than the overall average. A year earlier, in autumn 2004, the employment rate of those aged 50 to 69 was 54.3 per cent and the gap with the overall average 20.8 percentage points.

**There are currently around one million people in work who are over state pension age.**

26 www.EMETaskforce.gov.uk

**97.** SR2002 target rolled forward – PSA 4c: *Over the three years to spring 2006, increase the employment rate of people aged 50 and over and significantly reduce the difference between the employment rate of this group and the overall rate.*

## SR2002 Performance

**98.** The Department is **on course** to meet this target. The employment rate amongst those aged 50 to state pension age in autumn 2005 was 70.7 per cent and the gap with the overall average 4.0 per cent. Because of seasonal variation this is not directly comparable to the spring 2003 baseline, an employment rate of 70.0 per cent amongst people 50 to state pension age and a gap of 4.6 percentage points with the overall employment rate. As Figure 11 below illustrates, recent quarters have seen higher employment rates and lower gaps than the baseline. The employment rate has increased against a slightly unfavourable demographic change.

Figure 11 **Employment rates of people aged 50 to state pension age, those aged 16 to state pension age and the gap between the two**

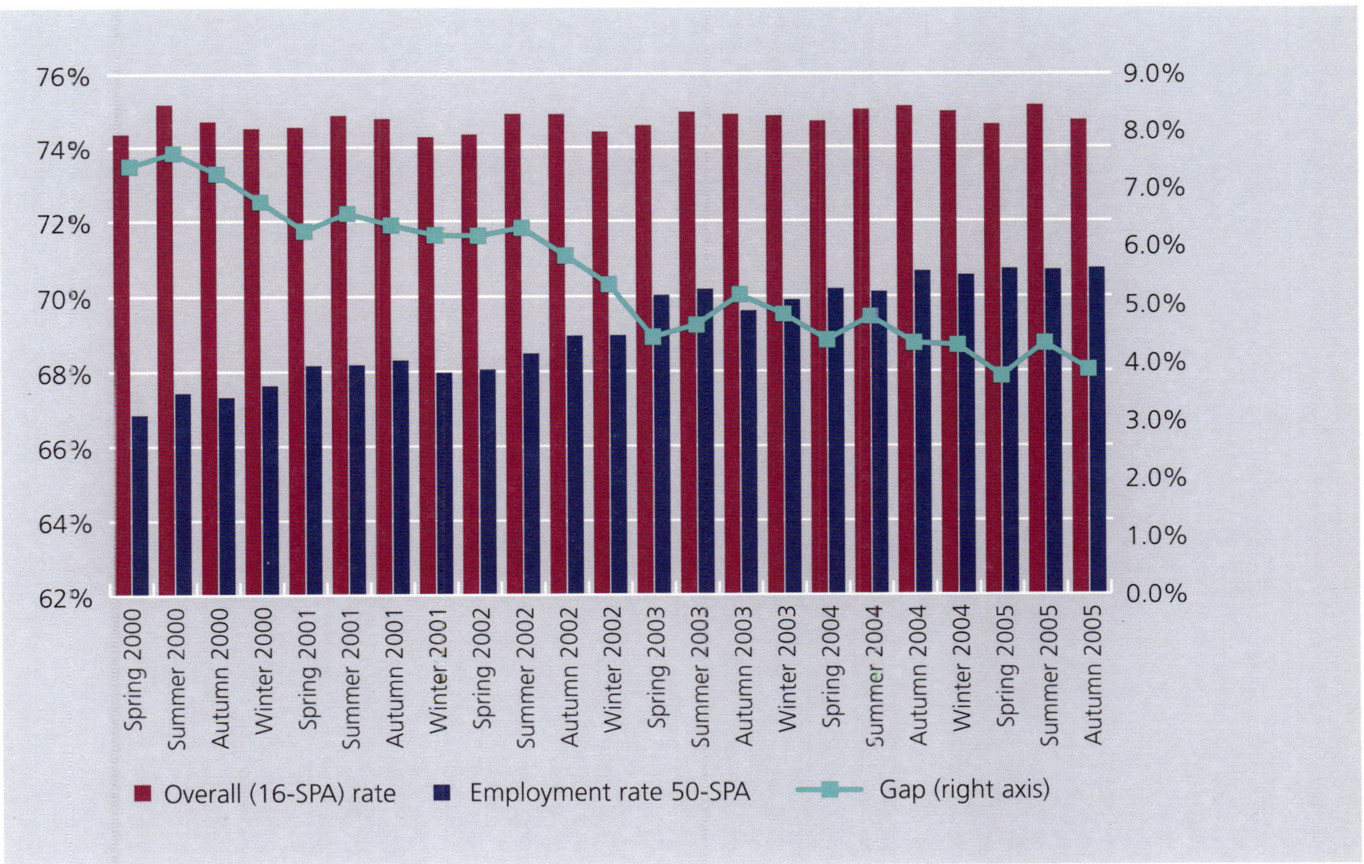

## Reasons for progress

- The continued strength of the GB labour market has provided a positive context for the Government's policies towards older workers.

- The New Deal 50 plus has supported over 150,000 job entries since April 2000. Back-to-work help is now available to people claiming Pension Credit (from age 60).

- The 'Age Positive' campaign has influenced employers by promoting the business case for age-diverse workforces, and every year sees increasing demand from employers for information about adopting non-ageist employment practices.

- Other developments have included more generous options for delaying taking State Pension, increasing numbers of individuals being issued with a pension forecast (see PSA 7a), and the publication of draft age discrimination regulations.

**PSA 4e: increase the employment rate of those with lowest qualifications and significantly reduce the difference between the employment rate of this group and the overall rate.**

## Measurement

**99.** The baseline is spring (March–May) 2005, when the employment rate for this group was 49.6 per cent and the gap with the overall employment rate was 25.1 percentage points.

**100.** A significant increase in the employment rate of the lowest qualified is defined in the PSA Technical note[27] as at least a one percentage point increase in the Spending Review period. Similarly, the gap with the overall rate has to close by at least one percentage point for the reduction to be significant.

## Performance

**101.** Performance against this target is **on course**. The employment rate for the 15 per cent lowest qualified for autumn 2005 is 51.1 per cent, and the employment gap is 23.6 percentage points. Although performance is typically high in autumn, Government Actuary's Department projections show that by spring 2008 the employment rate for this group is expected to be 51.9 per cent, which exceeds the SR2004 target by more than one percentage point.

**102.** Figure 12 illustrates actual and projected progress.

**103. SR2002 target rolled forward – PSA 4d:** *Over the three years to spring 2006, increase the employment rate of people with the lowest qualifications and significantly reduce the difference*

**27** www.dwp.gov.uk/publications/dwp/2004/psa/tech_note_2005_2008.pdf

*between the employment rate of this group and the overall rate.*

### SR2002 Performance

**104.** The target employment rate for spring 2006 is 51.2 per cent and the target employment gap is 23.4 percentage points. Current performance is therefore on course to meet, and slightly exceed, this target.

### Reasons for progress

**105.** The Department expects to meet this target largely through positive demographic effects of a downward trend in the proportion of the working-age population with no qualifications. People with some qualifications have much higher employment rates than those with no qualifications so, as the proportion of people with no qualifications falls, this target group is increasingly made up of people with some qualifications.

**106.** The Department has an evidence-based strategy for increasing the employment rate of those with no qualifications. This includes reinforcing the 'work first' approach, seeing work as the best route out of welfare, alongside better identification of those for whom lack of skills is a barrier to employment.

**107.** Existing tools include the development of coaching through the New Deal for Skills and the Adult Learning Option; as well as the screening of all customers to find those who need Basic Skills and English for Speakers of Other Languages courses.

**108.** Increasing the level of skills in the workforce is good for the economy as a whole, but consequently the people who remain in this group are increasingly harder to help.

Figure 12 **Employment rates and projections for the 15 per cent lowest qualified**

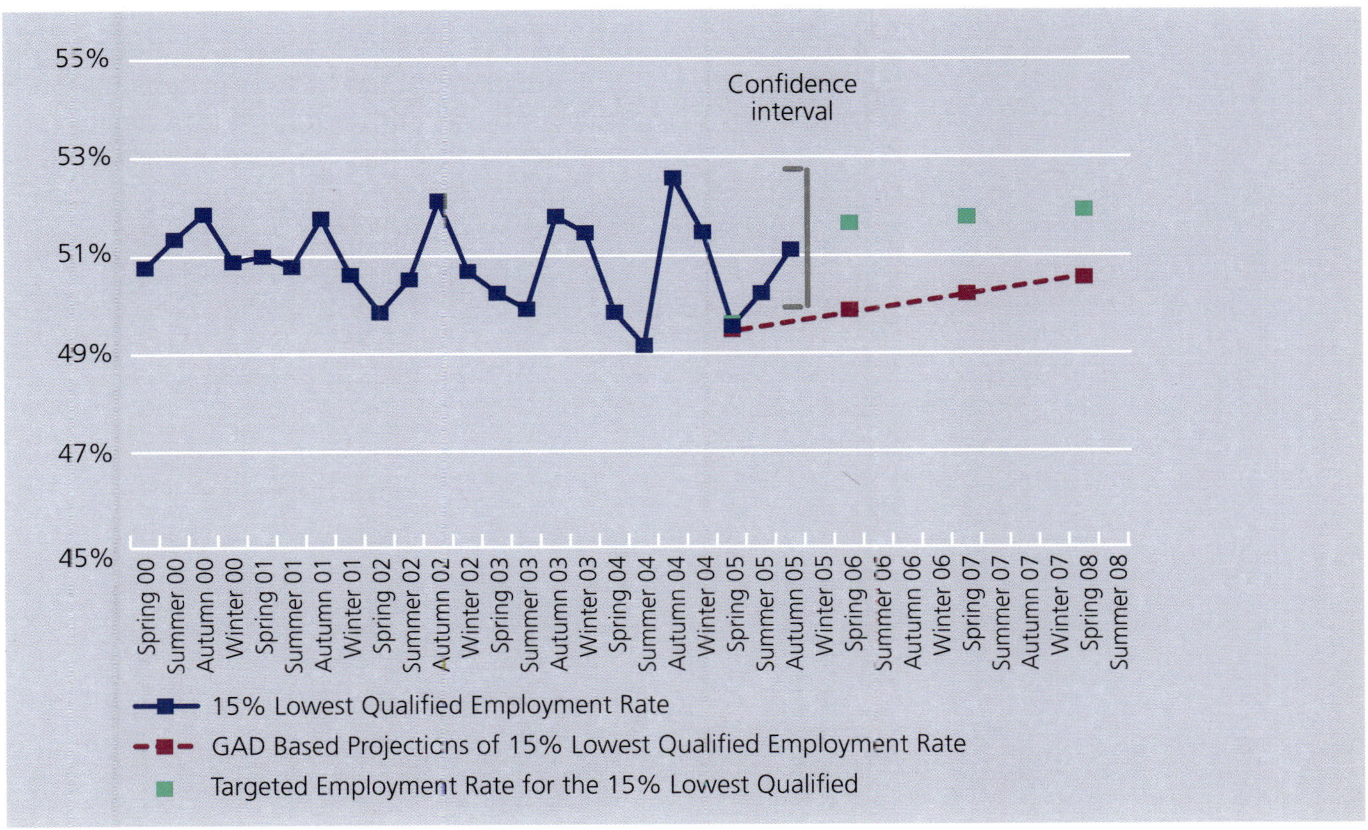

**PSA 4f: increase the employment rate of those living in local authority wards with the poorest initial labour market position and significantly reduce the difference between the employment rate of this group and the overall rate.**

## Measurement

**109.** The baseline is spring (March to May) 2005 when the employment rate for the most deprived wards was 59.7 per cent. The employment rate is based on ILO definitions, using estimates from the Labour Force Survey. Data is received quarterly and is not seasonally adjusted.

**110.** The baseline for SR 2002 PSA target 4e used a four-quarter average to minimise the impact of seasonality on performance. Changes to the way Labour Force Survey data is reported and the increasing robustness of quarter to quarter data mean that this target will now be measured on a quarter to quarter basis. This has the effect of greater fluctuations and variability.

**111.** A significant increase in the employment rate of people living in local authority wards with the poorest initial labour market position is defined in the PSA Technical Note[28] as at least a one percentage point increase in the Spending Review period. Similarly, the gap with the overall rate has to close by at least one percentage point for the reduction to be significant.

## Performance

**112.** Progress on this target is **not yet assessed**. Only a relatively short run of data after the baseline is available. An initial assessment will be based on spring 2006 data.

**113. SR2002 target rolled forward – PSA 4e:** *Over the three years to spring 2006, increase the employment rate of those living in local authority districts with the poorest initial labour market position and significantly reduce the difference between the employment rate of this group and the overall rate.*

## SR2002 Performance

**114.** Performance against this target is **on course**. After ten quarters, the employment rate of this group has increased by 2.8 percentage points over baseline and the gap has decreased by 3.2 percentage points. Latest available data shows that the employment rate within the 30 most deprived local authority districts in autumn 2005 was 66.4 per cent and the gap with the GB employment rate had fallen to 8.3 per cent. Continued progress at this rate would allow the target to be met comfortably.

**28** www.dwp.gov.uk/publications/dwp/2004/psa/tech_note_2005_2008.pdf

Figure 13 **Employment rates in the 30 local authority districts with the poorest initial labour market position**

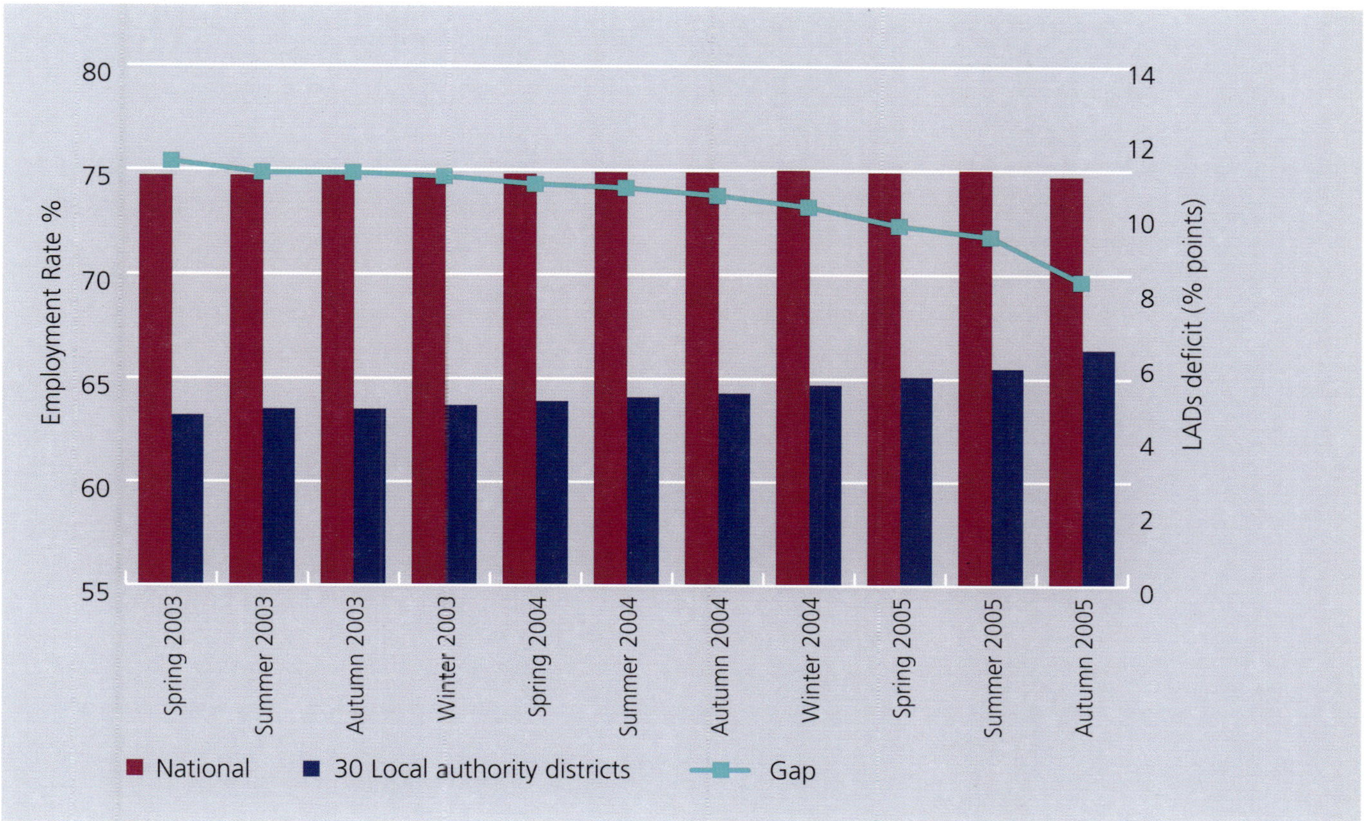


## Reasons for Progress

**115.** As with other aspects of social exclusion, worklessness varies widely across the country. While there is high employment in every region and across Great Britain, pockets of worklessness often exist close to more affluent areas and many highly successful labour markets. Rates of worklessness vary within regions and local authority districts and the Department has moved to a ward-based target in order to monitor these neighbourhood level 'pockets' effectively.

**116.** The position of deprived areas relative to the national position has improved gradually throughout recent years. Much of this reflects stable growth in the wider economy but this cannot be disentangled from policy initiatives which may have also had an impact.

**117.** The Department continues to provide locally-focused services, and will build on the lessons learned from Action Teams for Jobs and Working Neighbourhood Pilots in the development of the Cities Strategy.

**PSA target 5: By 2008 improve health and safety outcomes in Great Britain through progressive improvement in the control of risk in the workplace.**

**Further detail on this target is available in the Technical Note.[29]**

### Measurement

**118.** This target is measured by reference to a number of sub-targets, which are grouped under the two main areas of the Health and Safety Commission/Executive's work.

**119.** Progress towards the **conventional health and safety sub-targets[30]** is measured against a 2004–05 baseline when:

- the incidence rate of work-related fatal and major injuries was 118.4 per 100,000 workers;
- the incidence rate of self-reported work-related ill health was 1,800 per 100,000 workers (1.8 per cent); and
- the number of working days lost due to work-related injury and ill health was 1.5 per worker.

**120.** The **major hazards sub-targets** are measured against a 2001–02 baseline when:

- the number of events reported by licence holders which the Health and Safety Executive's Nuclear Installations Inspectorate judges as having the potential to challenge a nuclear safety system was 143;
- the number of major and significant hydrocarbon releases in the offshore oil and gas sector was 113; and
- the number of relevant RIDDOR[31] reportable dangerous occurences in the onshore sector was 179.

**121.** Data for monitoring this target is gathered from various sources:

- For the **conventional health and safety sub-targets**, sources include the Labour Force Survey; Self-reported Work-related Illness household surveys; the Health and Occupation Reporting network; and other reports made under RIDDOR. The Health and Safety Executive (HSE) publishes annual progress reports each autumn.[32]
- The three measures of conventional health and safety outcomes (work-related injuries, work-related ill health, working days lost) are subject to sampling error/statistical uncertainty. To maximise the ability to detect change, the judgement on progress is based on analysis of movements from all relevant data sources, including indicators of the control of risks in the workplace, as well as data from other sources.
- For the **major hazards sub-targets,** data is obtained from reports made to HSE for the nuclear and offshore sectors and relevant reports made under RIDDOR for the onshore sector.

**29** www.hse.gov.uk/aboutus/plans/sr2004.htm
**30** www.hse.gov.uk/revitalising/what_is/index.htm
**31** Reporting of Injuries, Diseases and Dangerous Occurrences Regulations
**32** www.hse.gov.uk/statistics/targets.htm

**122.** Data is collected quarterly and made public on the HSE's website. Progress is formally published annually in the Health and Safety Commission's Annual Report.

**Performance**

**123.** Assessment of progress for the overall target is **not yet assessed**.

**124.** The major hazards element of the PSA is on course. The 2004–05 baseline for the conventional health and safety element was only established in November 2005.[33] However, HSE hopes to maintain the encouraging progress highlighted by the 2004–05 statistics (with the SR2000 ill health and days lost targets 'probably' and 'possibly met' and encouraging signs on injuries).

**125.** To monitor progress, HSE will use its established statistical sources as well as developing a new programme of workplace health and safety surveys to provide details of work-related ill health and injury in the context of working conditions and the management of health and safety.

Figure 14 **Conventional health and safety sub-targets and performance**

| Sub-target | Baselines: 2004–05 | 2007–08 target |
|---|---|---|
| Injuries | 118.4 injuries per 100,000 employees | 3 per cent reduction |
| Ill health incidence | 1,800 per 100,000 employed* | 6 per cent reduction |
| Days lost | 1.5 days lost per worker | 9 per cent reduction |

* Based on self-reporting surveys. Assessment of progress will use other sources too.

Figure 15 **Major hazards sub-targets and performance**

| Sub-target | Baselines: 2001–02 | Outturn to Q4 2005–06* | 2007–08 target |
|---|---|---|---|
| Nuclear industries | 143 | 118 | 7.5 per cent reduction |
| Offshore hazardous installations | 113 | 73 | 45 per cent reduction |
| Onshore hazardous installations | 179 | 130 | 15 per cent reduction |

* Latest figures

33 www.hse.gov.uk/statistics/overall/hssh0405.pdf

Figure 16 **Performance trajectory for nuclear industries**

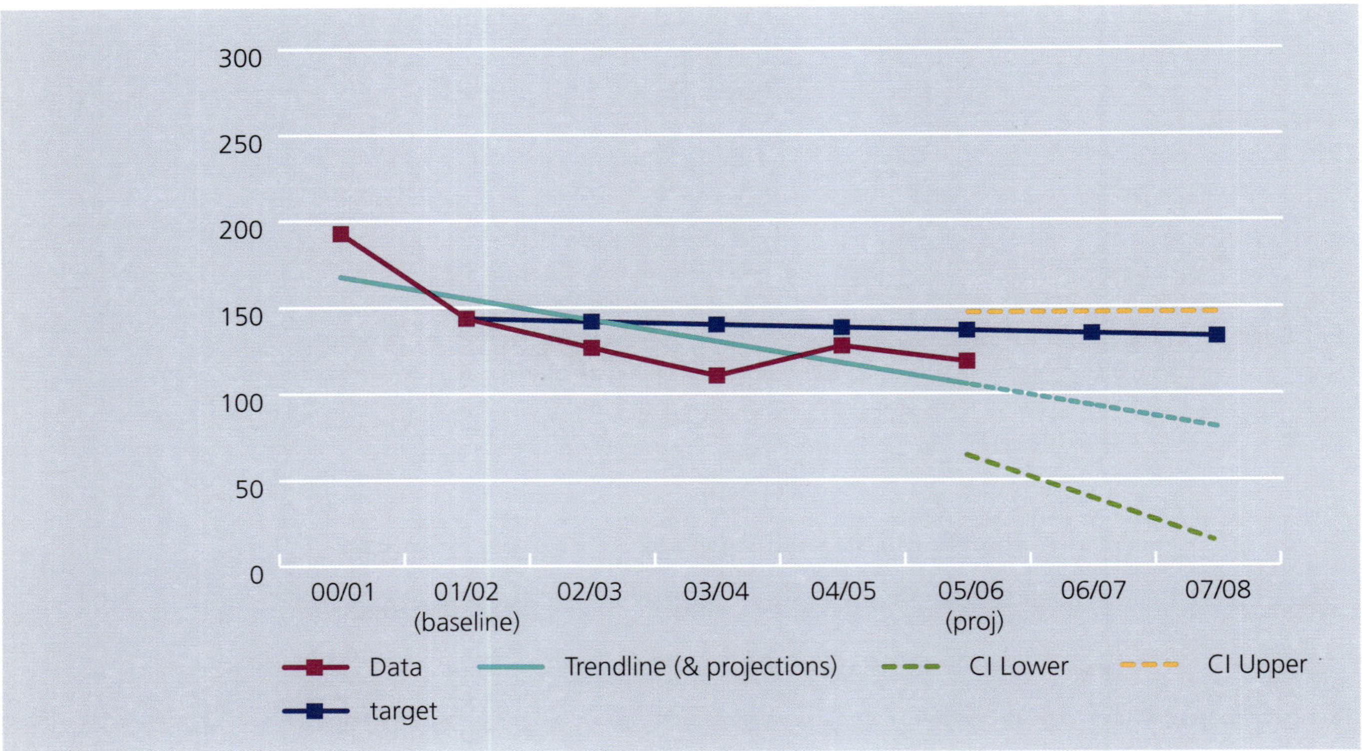


Figure 17 **Performance trajectory for offshore hazardous installations**

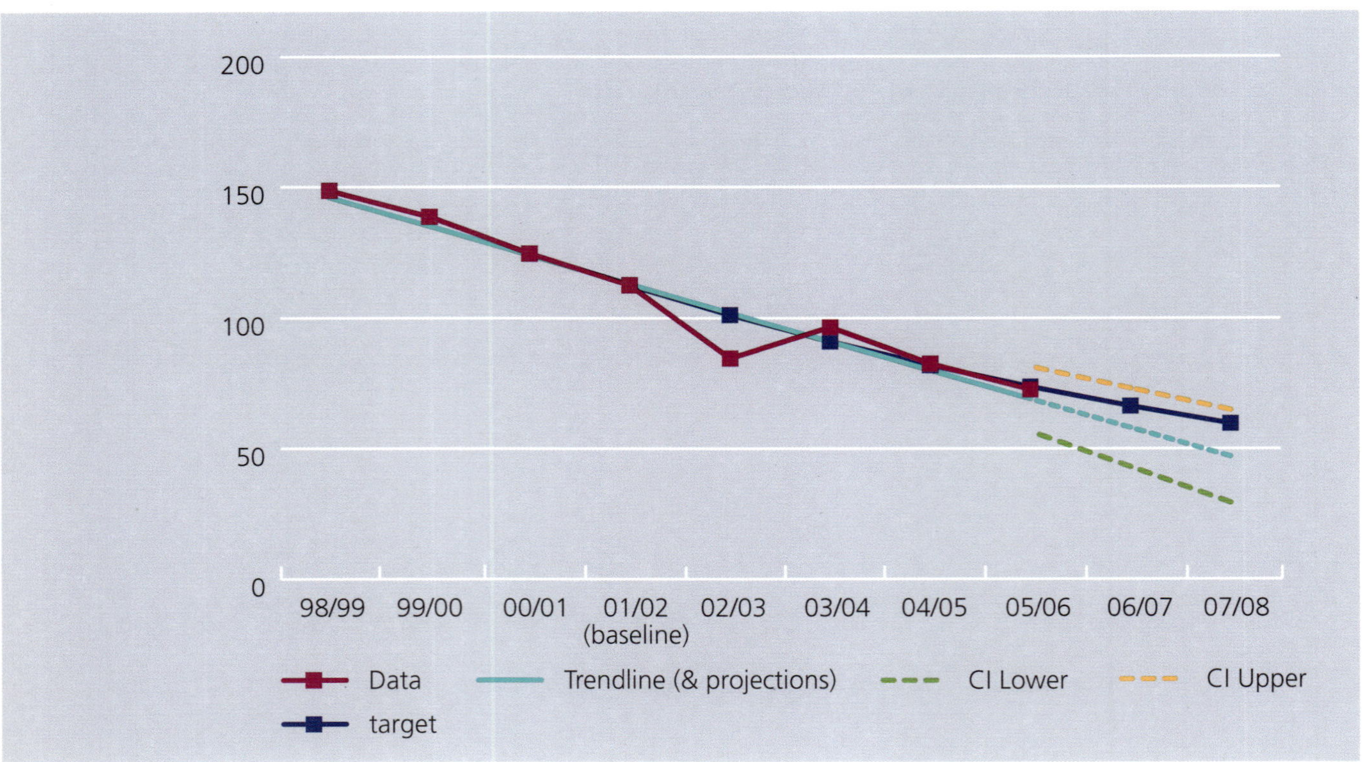

Figure 18 **Performance trajectory for onshore hazardous installations**

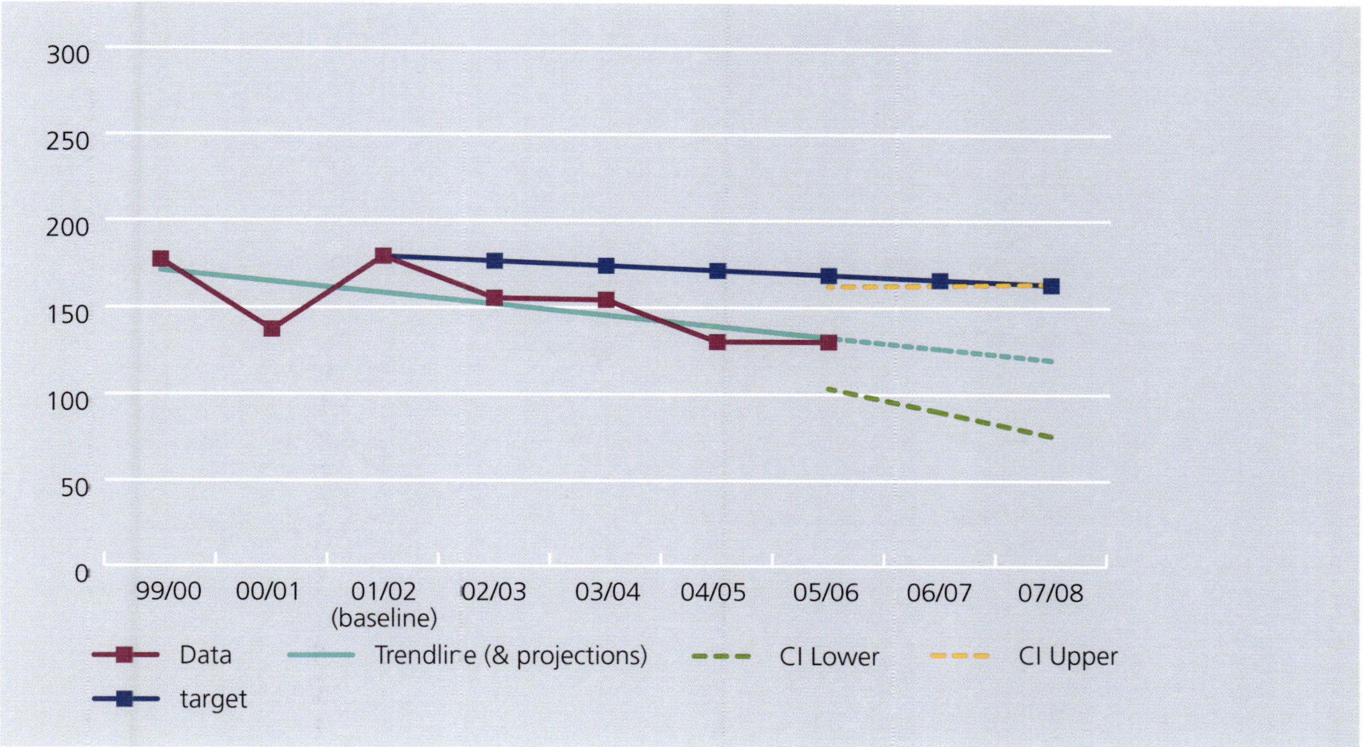


## Reasons for progress

### Conventional health and safety

**126.** The 2004–05 statistics show encouraging progress on the incidence of work-related ill health, numbers of days lost due to work-related illness and injury, and rates of fatal and major injury in the construction industry. This indicates that HSE's long-term approach to delivering improved health and safety outcomes (now incorporated within the Fit3 Strategic Programme) is beginning to have an impact. The scale of the challenge remains considerable, but it is hoped these trends will be maintained through activities such as:

- working with the Department for Work and Pensions and the Department of Health to implement the new Health, Work and Well-being strategy, which focuses on improving the health and well-being of working-age people;

- supporting the Ministerial Task Force in changing public sector management culture and thereby reducing numbers of working days lost;

- providing occupational health advice to small and medium sized enterprises in England and Wales through Workplace Health Connect, with a pathfinder service that began in February 2006;

- communicating to reduce incidence of back pain at work. The 'Backs! 2005' campaign promoted the use of lifting and mechanical aids and will be supported by a further publicity and enforcement campaign in 2006; and
- engaging and supporting local authority colleagues to tackle priority areas in the sectors they enforce.

### Major hazards

**127.** The Major Hazards Strategic Programme is making good progress. Numbers of precursor incidents continue to decline and HSE is on course to deliver the sub-targets. Catastrophic incidents remain rare events.

**The 2004–05 statistics show encouraging progress on the incidence of work-related ill health, numbers of days lost due to work-related illness and injury.**

**128.** Key achievements within the major hazards programme that are considered to have affected performance are:

- Developing successful partnership initiatives with key stakeholders in securing commitment to:
  - voluntary reporting of uncontrolled releases of flammable and toxic gases;
  - establishing new performance indicators for the effectiveness of measures to control major hazard risks; and
  - using the Safety Significance Rating System for nuclear and radiological events on licensed civil nuclear sites and providing HSE with consolidated performance data.
- Implementing a joint HSE/industry intervention programme to improve installation integrity and reduce uncontrolled hydrocarbon releases offshore.
- Maintaining safety standards during the reorganisation of the national gas distribution network by applying the gas safety case assessment regime sensibly.

# PART THREE **SECURITY IN RETIREMENT**

**Objective: to combat poverty and promote security and independence in retirement for today's and tomorrow's pensioners.**

**PSA target 6:** By 2008, be paying Pension Credit to at least 3.2 million pensioner households, while maintaining a focus on the most disadvantaged by ensuring that at least 2.2 million of these households are in receipt of the Guarantee Credit.

### Measurement

**129.** Until September 2005, progress against this target was measured using information from the Pension Credit Quarterly Statistical Enquiry[34], which held information on the numbers and characteristics of Pension Credit recipients. From October 2005 the Quarterly Statistical Enquiry was replaced by a 100 per cent data source which now forms the basis of the majority of the Department's National Statistics. This data source is subject to validation by the National Audit Office.

**130.** Further information on this target can be found in the PSA Technical Note.[35]

### Performance

**131.** There is some **slippage** towards the target of paying at least 3.2 million households by 2008. However, the Department is **on course** to ensure that 2.2 million households receive the Guarantee Credit. At the end of February 2006, 2.7 million households were receiving Pension Credit; 2.1 million of whom received the Guarantee Credit.

**132.** Figure 19 overleaf shows how the number of households receiving Pension Credit has grown since its introduction in October 2003.

**133. SR2002 target rolled forward – PSA 6:** *by 2006, be paying Pension Credit to at least 3 million pensioner households.*

### SR2002 Performance

**134.** This target will **not** have been **met**. Final figures will not be available until July 2006 but published early estimates indicate that 2.7 million households were receiving Pension Credit at the end of February 2006.

**135.** It is more challenging to reach those entitled to smaller amounts or to the Savings Credit only, who may be less familiar with the entitlement available to them. Analysis, derived from the Family Resources Survey, indicates that 31 per cent of those customers who fail to take up Savings Credit only would be entitled to less than £5 a week if they did so.

**34** www.dwp.gov.uk/asd/pcqse.asp
**35** www.dwp.gov.uk/publications/dwp/2004/psa/tech_note_2005_2008.pdf

Figure 19 **Households in receipt of Pension Credit**

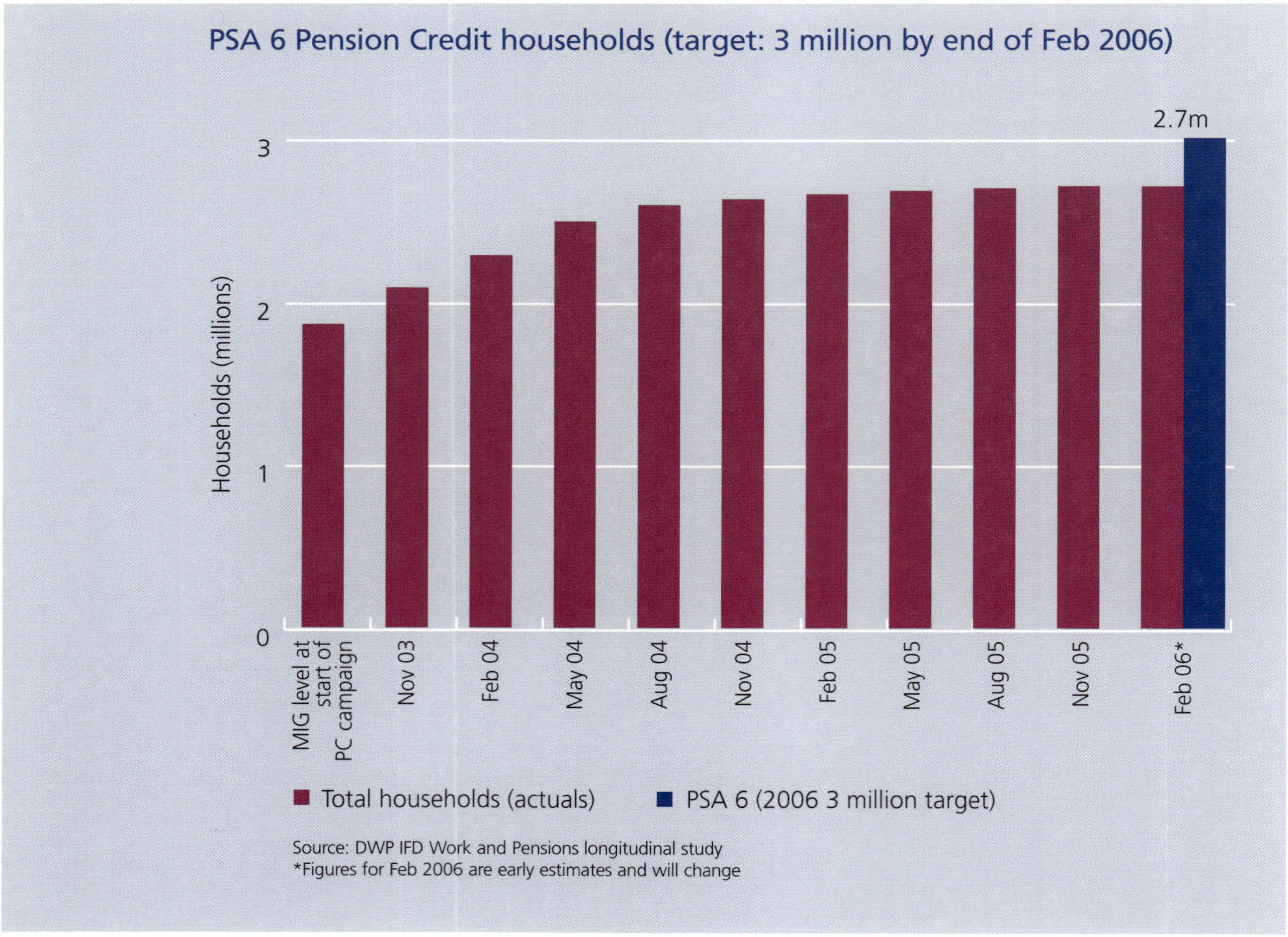


## Improving performance

**136.** The Pension Service is committed to improving take-up. It is continually looking at further ways to identify those who may be entitled and encouraging them to apply.

- Data matching is helping to identify people who are likely to be entitled to Pension Credit but are not claiming, so that The Pension Service can approach them and encourage them to take up their entitlements.
- The Pension Service has written to every pensioner household to tell them about Pension Credit.
- Over the six months from 17 October 2005, a direct mail initiative 'You're Missing Out' was targeted at 1.5 million people who were most likely to be entitled to Pension Credit. These mailshots were supported by national and regional press activity.

- The Pension Service Local Service visited around 23,000 people likely to be entitled to Pension Credit every week, providing advice on a wide range of benefits, not just Pension Credit.
- Since 5 December 2005, customers who contact the Pension Credit Application Line to apply for Pension Credit have been able to claim Housing Benefit and Council Tax Benefit during the same phone call, using a new shortened three-page claim form.

**PSA target 7:** Improve working-age individuals' awareness of their retirement provision such that by 2007–08, 15.4 million individuals are regularly issued a pension forecast and 60,000 successful pension traces are undertaken a year.

**PSA 7a:** by 2007–08, 15.4 million individuals are regularly issued a pension forecast.

### Measurement

**137.** The baseline for measuring this target is spring 2005. The target will be met if 15.4 million individuals are issued with at least one of four types of pension forecast[36] in the three-year period from the beginning of April 2005 to end of March 2008. Progress is monitored by reference to monthly reports from the forecast-issuing IT systems.

**138.** Further information can be found in the PSA Technical Note.[37]

### Performance

**139.** The Department is **on course** to reach the target. Between April 2005 and the end of March 2006, a total of 12,918,659 forecasts have been issued. This equates to 12,279,266 individuals being issued with at least one of the four forecast types. This represents progress of 79 per cent towards the target of 15.4 million individuals regularly receiving a forecast. Figure 20 shows progress towards the target – it shows anticipated levels of achievement at each year end along with the actual volumes achieved

**36** Combined Pension Forecasts (CPFs), Automatic Pension Forecasts (APFs), Individual Pension Forecasts (IPFs) or Real Time Pension Forecasts (RTPFs).

**37** www.dwp.gov.uk/publications/dwp/2004/psa/tech_note_2005_2008.pdf

by the end of each quarter to date and reflects the position at the end of March 2006. The figures are for all forecast types.

**140.** Progress towards the target is expected to level off, as it becomes increasingly difficult to find 'new' people who have yet to receive a first forecast during the PSA period. (An individual can only be counted once, no matter how many forecasts they receive).

### Reasons for progress

- The Pension Service has been successful in persuading employers and pension providers to issue Combined Pension Forecasts. and has exceeded the anticipated Automatic Pension Forecast (APF) volumes for 2005–06. A total of 8.7 million individuals received an APF, against a target of 8 million.

Figure 20 **Number of pension forecasts issued since June 2005**

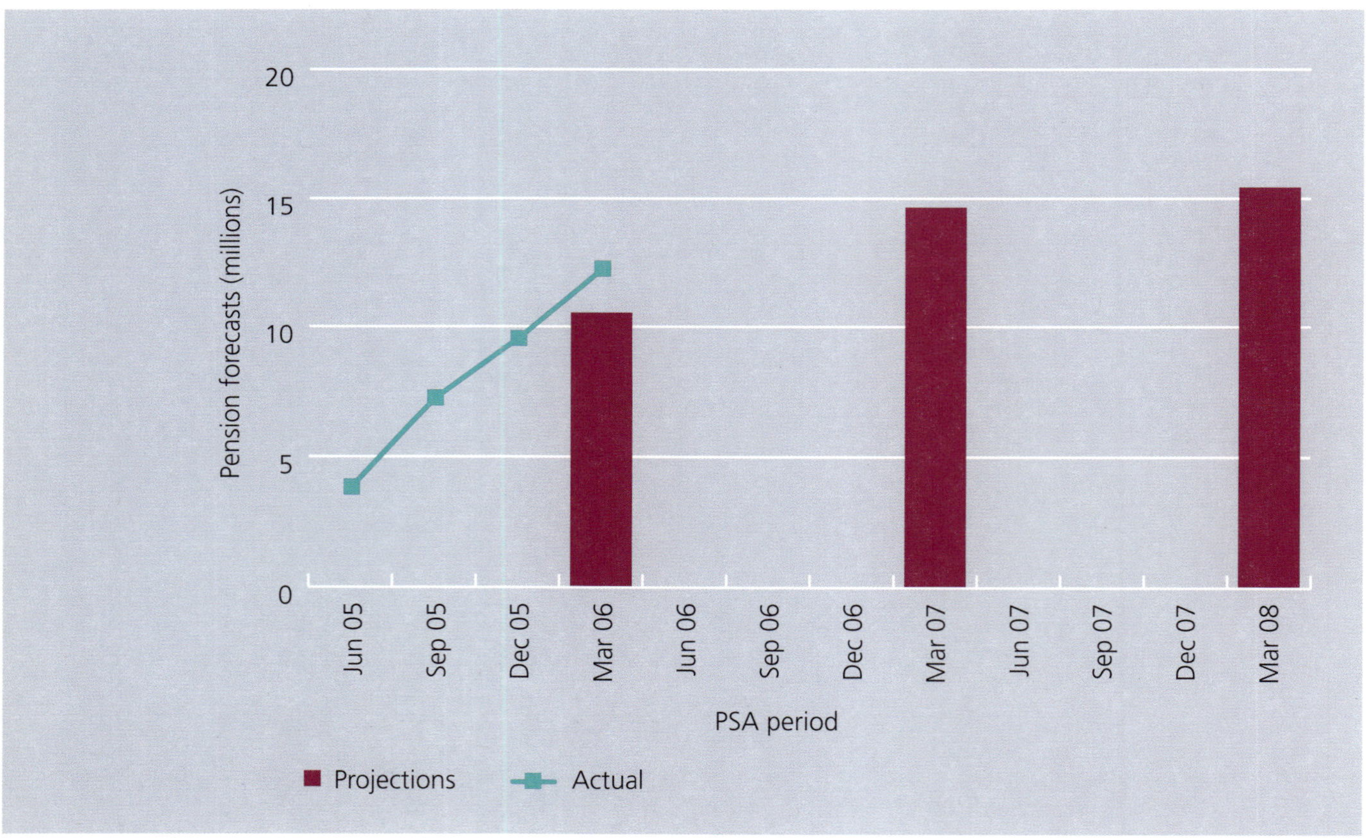

**PSA 7b: by 2007–08, 60,000 successful pension traces are undertaken a year**

### Measurement

**141.** The Pension Tracing Service became part of the Department for Work and Pensions from April 2005. Prior to this the service was delivered by the Occupational Pensions Regulatory Authority (Opra). Figures from the Opra annual report and accounts 2004–05 show that 25,200 requests were received and 95 per cent of these were successfully traced.

**142.** Further information can be found in the PSA Technical Note.[38]

**143.** The Pension Tracing Service is administered by The Pension Service on behalf of the Department. It collects data on the number of callers, the number of traces and the number of successful traces.

### Performance

**144.** Performance against this target is **not yet assessed**, since formal assessment is not required until 2007–08. However, statistics indicate that the Pension Tracing Service undertook 30,619 successful traces in 2005–06 – a 20 per cent increase on the number achieved in the previous year.

### Reasons for progress

**145.** This is a challenging but achievable target. Increased marketing of the Pension Tracing Service should succeed in raising its profile, encouraging greater numbers of people to approach it with requests for help.

**The Pension Service has written to every pensioner household to tell them about Pension Credit.**

**38** www.dwp.gov.uk/publications/dwp/2004/psa/tech_note_2005_2008.pdf

# PART FOUR **DISABLED PEOPLE**

**Objective: to improve rights and opportunities for disabled people in a fair and inclusive society.**

**PSA target 8:** In the three years to March 2008:

- further improve the rights of disabled people and remove barriers to their participation in society, working with other government departments, including through increasing awareness of the rights of disabled people;
- increase the employment rate of disabled people, taking account of the economic cycle; and
- significantly reduce the difference between their employment rate and the overall rate, taking account of the economic cycle.

**PSA 8a:** further improve the rights of disabled people and remove barriers to their participation in society, working with other government departments, including through increasing awareness of the rights of disabled people.

### Measurement

**146.** The measure used to detect an improvement in the rights of disabled people is the percentage of adults who are aware that the civil rights of disabled people are protected. The baseline is October 2004–March 2005 when 73.4 per cent of adults fell in this category. This information is collected continuously from the Office for National Statistics Omnibus Survey[39] from October 2004 and is available for analysis eight times a year.

**147.** An increase of two percentage points in the measure, between October 2004 and March 2008, is expected to be statistically significant with 95 per cent confidence. Further detail on this target is available from the PSA Technical Note.[40]

**148.** The current PSA target records the rise in awareness in the general population of the civil rights of disabled people over the period covered by SR 2004. This represents a substantial modification to the previous target, agreed in SR 2002, which was designed to monitor progress in implementing the Government's commitment to legislate to improve the civil rights of disabled people and to monitor other progress, including media and other campaigns to raise awareness.

### Performance

**149.** Between April and September 2005 awareness of disability rights is estimated at 72.7 per cent. This is below the baseline value of 73.4 per cent, therefore this target is displaying **slippage**.

39 www.statistics.gov.uk/services/SurveyOmnibus.asp
40 www.dwp.gov.uk/publications/dwp/2004/psa/tech_note_2005_2008.pdf

**Improving performance**
**150.** The Department did not conduct any significant awareness-raising activity between April and September 2005, the period covered by the latest available data. In December 2005, the Department launched an awareness-raising campaign, which will run until May 2006.

**151.** The Department will plan the next phase of awareness-raising activity following research on the impact of the current campaign.

**152. SR2002 target rolled forward – PSA 7b:** *In the three years to 2006, work to improve the rights of disabled people and to remove barriers to their participation in society.*

**SR2002 Performance**
**153. Final assessment:** This target has been **met.** The specific objectives of the SR2002 target have now been achieved. The Department is continuing to improve the rights of disabled people and to remove barriers to their participation in society, in working to meet its SR2004 target.

**Reasons for progress**
**154.** The Department employs four strategies in working to achieve PSA target 8a:

**Further improve the rights of disabled people**
**155.** The Disability Discrimination Act 2005 provisions are being progressively implemented from December 2005. These include:

- providing protection, by amendments to the definition of disability, to a further 250,000 people who have HIV infection, cancer or multiple sclerosis, effectively from the point of diagnosis; and

- making it unlawful for private clubs (with 25 or more members) to treat disabled people and guests less favourably, and for locally electable bodies to treat their disabled members less favourably.

**156.** The new Disability Equality Duty on the public sector will come into force in December 2006, requiring public authorities to give due regard to the need to promote equality of opportunity for disabled people in the way they conduct their business. The regulations and statutory Code of Practice relating to this requirement came into force in December 2005.

**157.** The Department has also promoted disability rights internationally, including:

- a major UK Presidency Ministerial conference on disability in November 2005 which drew attention to good practice across the EU in the areas of routinely taking account of disability in formulating policy and promoting independence; and

- a joint Department for Work and Pensions and Foreign Office team led the EU negotiations in August 2005 on the UN Convention on Disability Rights and secured important improvements to the text. A subsequent meeting in January 2006 enhanced the text further.

### Proactive awareness raising

**158.** The Department launched an awareness-raising campaign on the Disability Discrimination Act in December 2005. This campaign was designed to meet the specific needs of small and medium-size enterprises, business intermediaries and the general public. Agencies with a suitable background in both disability issues and communicating with small employers have been contracted to undertake public relations and advertising work in support of the campaign.

**159.** In addition, in early 2006, the Disability Rights Commission launched an awareness-raising campaign to challenge negative attitudes to disability.

### Sponsor organisations that improve opportunities of disabled people

**160.** The Department continues to work closely with the Disability Rights Commission and to monitor the Commission's performance through regular meetings. Progress during 2005–06 in this area includes:

- 93,743 contacts handled by the Disability Rights Commission's Helpline between 1 April 2005 and 31 March 2006;
- 129 cases referred to the Disability Conciliation Service while the Commission directly funded 54 new legal cases and made three further interventions in the Higher Courts;
- the launch of a 'Disability Debate' which is intended to produce a longer term agenda for disability and disability rights; and
- issue of the Disability Equality Duty Codes of Practice.

**161.** Plans to create a Commission for Equality and Human Rights (CEHR) are on course for the new body to open in October 2007. The CEHR will bring together the work of the three existing equality commissions (including the Disability Rights Commission) and take responsibility for new laws in respect of age, religion or belief, and sexual orientation. The Equality Act 2006 provides for distinct governance arrangements for disability in the CEHR which will ensure that the focus on the disability agenda is maintained.

### Cross-government work on further increasing opportunities for disabled people

**162.** The Department is leading the Government's long-term strategy for disabled people and cross-government implementation of the Strategy Unit report *Improving the Life Chances of Disabled People*.[41] In December 2005, it set up a new Office for Disability Issues (ODI)[42] to drive forward this work in partnership with other departments, in particular the Department for Education and Skills, the Department of Health and the Office of the Deputy Prime Minister.

**41** www.strategy.gov.uk/downloads/work_areas/disability/disability-report/index.htm
**42** www.officefordisability.gov.uk

**163.** The ODI will act as focal point for disability across Government. Its aims include:

- influencing and challenging government from within;
- agreeing a cross-government plan for delivering equality for disabled people;
- working directly with disabled people and organisations to identify barriers and solutions, and to champion innovative projects; and
- providing a source of expertise and information on disability.

**164.** The ODI and other government departments are also implementing a range of recommendations in the Strategy Unit report, including Individual Budget pilots (led by the Department of Health), aiming to give older and disabled people more choice and control over their lives.

**PSA 8b and c: taking account of the economic cycle, increase the employment rate of disabled people and significantly reduce the difference between their employment rate and the overall rate.**

## Measurement

**165.** The baseline for this target is spring 2005, when the employment rate of disabled people was 46.6 per cent, and the gap between their rate and the overall rate was 28.0 percentage points.

**166.** The definition of a disability for the purpose of the SR2002 PSA includes people with a disability consistent with the Disability Discrimination Act (DDA) and/or people with a long term work-limiting disability. For the purpose of SR2004, the definition of a disability has changed and only includes those people with a disability consistent with the DDA.

**167.** Excluding those with a work-limiting disability has the important implication of lowering the monitored PSA employment rate. The definition of disability supporting the employment elements of this target was changed between SR2002 and SR2004 in order to reduce measurement problems that arose from variations in reported disability in the Labour Force Survey (LFS) for those with a work-limiting disability only.

**168.** The target is monitored quarterly using ILO employment rates from the LFS. Because data is not seasonally adjusted, comparisons can only be made year on year.

**169.** Further information can be found in the PSA Technical Note.[43]

## Performance

**170.** Performance against this target is **not yet assessed**. The first assessment will use spring 2006 data which will be available in July 2006.

**171. SR2002 target rolled forward – PSA 7a:** *In the three years to spring 2006, increase the employment rate of disabled people, taking account of the economic cycle, and significantly reduce the difference between their employment rate and the overall rate.*

## SR2002 Performance

**172.** Progress is **on course** to meet this target. The base year for measuring this target was spring 2003 when the employment rate of disabled people was 48.9 per cent and the gap between this rate and the overall employment rate was 25.6 percentage points. By spring 2005, the employment rate of disabled people was 50.1 per cent, an increase of 1.1 percentage points. Over the same period, the gap in employment rates has narrowed by 1.1 percentage points to 24.5 per cent.

**173.** The general trend is that the disabled employment rate is going up, while the gap between the overall employment rate and the disabled employment rate is going down.

Figure 21 **Employment rates of disabled people, GB overall rate and gap between the two**

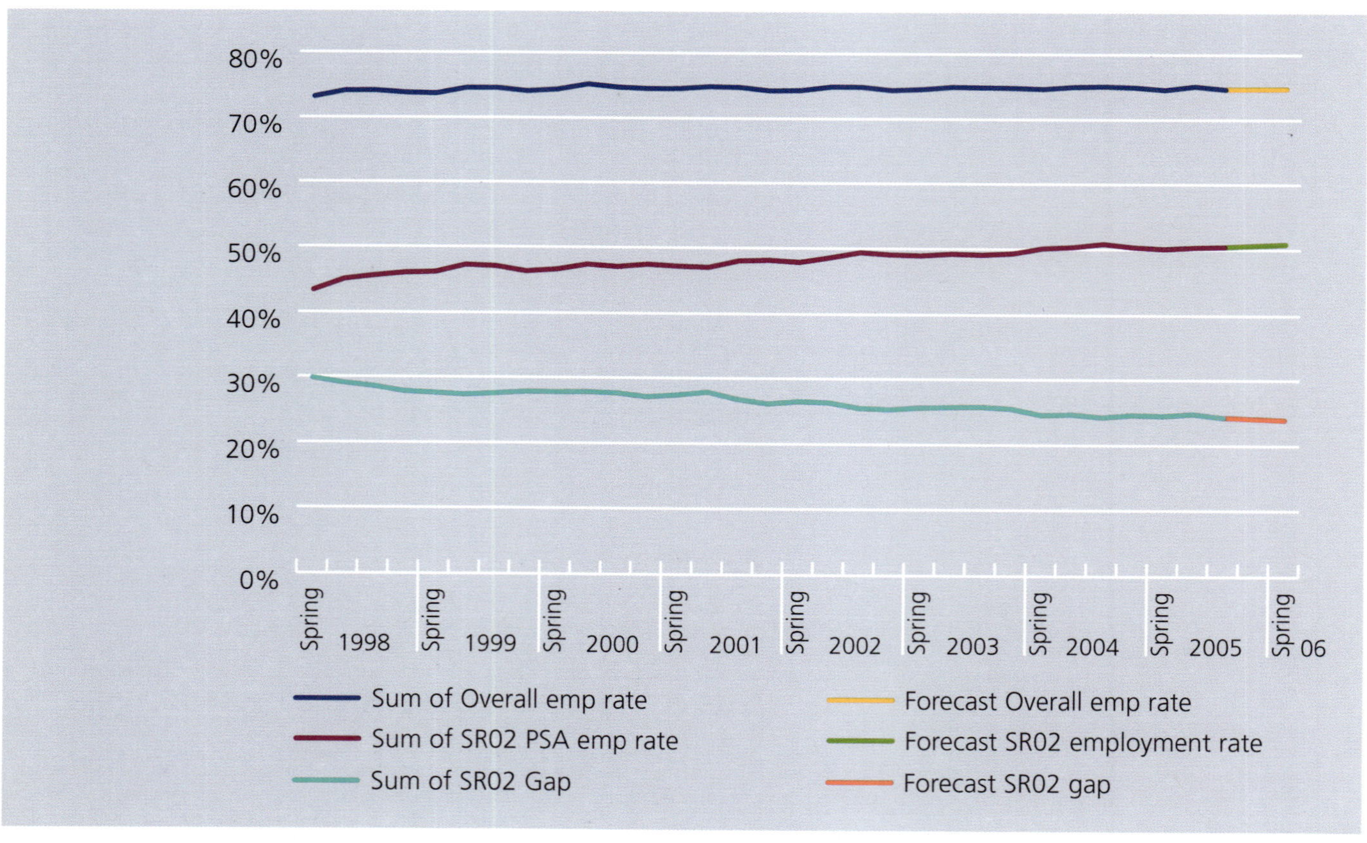


43 www.dwp.gov.uk/publications/dwp/2004/psa/tech_note_2005_2008.pdf

**Reasons for progress**

**174.** Some of the increase in the employment rate is due to a general trend in the population to report milder disabilities or health conditions. In the last five years the number of disabled people has increased by half a million to 5.7 million. This includes those already in work; accordingly this trend has led to an increase in the percentage of disabled people who are in work, which reduces the gap between the overall employment rate and the employment rate for disabled people.

**175.** Work-focused interviews, the Incapacity Benefits Pathways pilots, and the New Deal for Disabled People are also likely to have had a small positive effect upon the employment rate of disabled people.

**In the last five years the number of disabled people has increased by half a million to 5.7 million.**

# PART FIVE **QUALITY OF SERVICE DELIVERY**

**Objective: to ensure customers receive a high quality service, including levels of accuracy.**

**PSA target 9:** Improve Housing Benefit administration by:

- reducing the average time taken to process a Housing Benefit claim to no more than 48 days nationally and across the bottom 15 per cent of local authorities to no more than 55 days, by March 2008;
- increasing the number of cases in the deregulated private rented sector in receipt of Local Housing Allowance to 740,000 by 2008; and
- increasing the number of cases in receipt of the Local Housing Allowance where the rent is paid directly to the claimant to 470,000 by 2008.

**PSA 9a:** reduce the average time taken to process a Housing Benefit claim to no more than 48 days nationally and across the bottom 15 per cent of local authorities to no more than 55 days, by March 2008.

### Measurement

**176.** The baseline for measuring this target is 2002–03 when the average time taken to process a Housing Benefit/Council Tax Benefit claim nationally was 55 days. In the same period, processing a Housing Benefit/Council Tax Benefit claim across the bottom 15 per cent of local authorities took an average of 99 days.

**177.** The target will be measured using Housing Benefit/Council Tax Benefit Management Information annual un-audited data, available three months after the end of each reporting year and will be monitored on a quarterly basis.[44] The data is submitted by local authorities and demonstrates reported performance. It is not compulsory to return the data, but most local authorities do so.

**178.** Further information can be found in the PSA Technical Note.[45]

### Performance

**179.** Performance against the national average target for all local authorities is **ahead** of expectations. This has been achieved through a long-term programme of reform, engagement and support. Figure 22 shows that by year-ending 31 March 2005, the target had been exceeded with claims taking an average of 46 days to process. Data for the year to December 2005 demonstrates that performance has continued to improve with these indicative figures[46] showing an average of 36 days to process a claim.

**180.** For the bottom 15 per cent of local authorities, performance has remained **on course**. Local authorities in this group have been making good progress, with new claims being processed in an average of 76 days during year ending 31 March

**44** www.dwp.gov.uk/asd/asd1/hb_ctb/performance.asp.
**45** www.dwp.gov.uk/publications/dwp/2004/psa/tech_note_2005_2008.pdf
**46** The target is measured against annual performance and any quarterly information should only be used as a guide.

2005. Data for the year to December 2005 demonstrates that performance has continued to improve with these indicative figures[47] showing an average of 56 days to process a claim.

**181.** When interpreting Figure 22 it is important to remember that the target is measured against the annual performance, and the year-to-date information is used as a guide to what the annual performance figure is likely to attain.

## Reasons for progress

**182.** Poorly performing local authorities are targeted through performance standards funding (£200 million fund under SR2002) and the Department undertakes risk-based engagements, inspections, and provision of consultancy support with poorer local authorities. This, alongside the effect of benefit reforms to streamline the claims process is likely to have greatly contributed to the improvement in reported performance.

Figure 22 **Processing times for Housing Benefit and Council Tax Benefit claims**

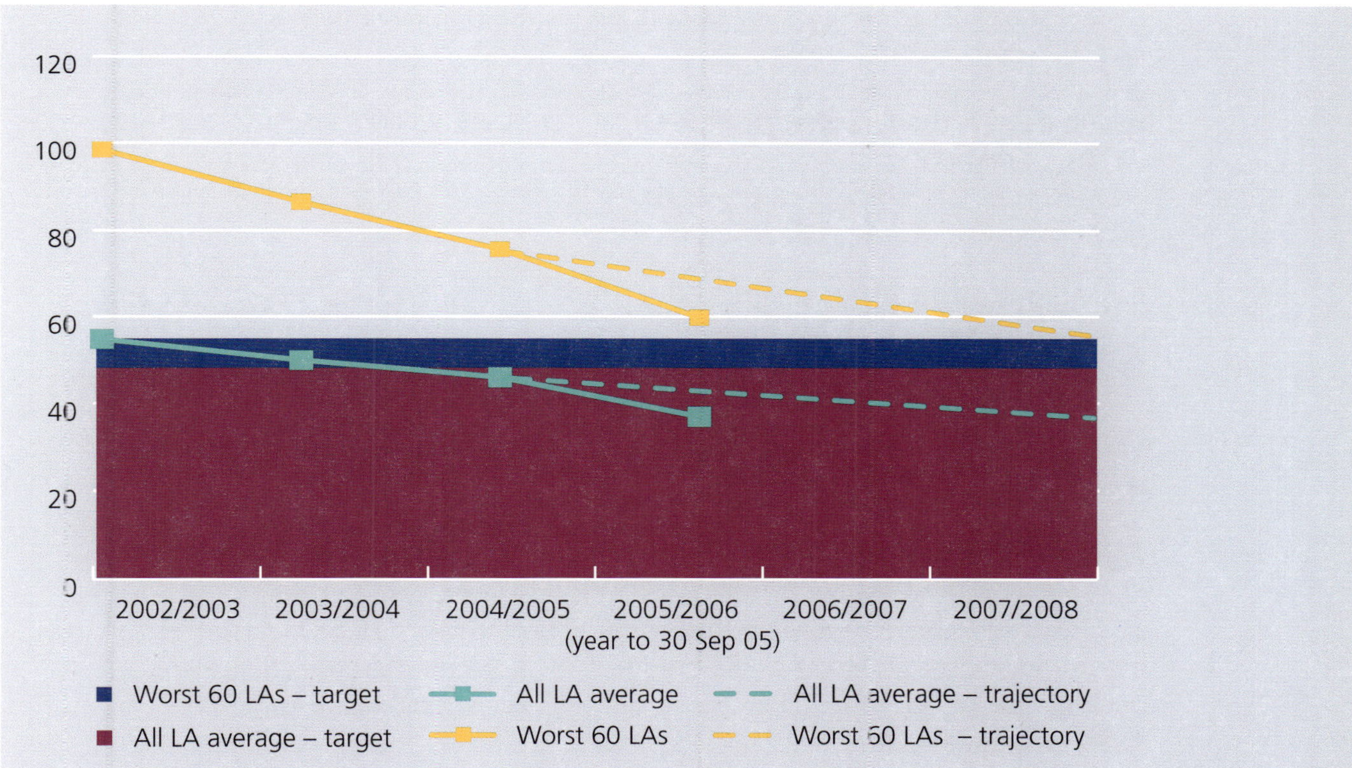


Data source: Housing Benefit Management Information System stats 124 data.
Notes:
(1) Local authorities has been abbreviated to 'LAs'.
(2) Data is reported performance from LAs.
(3) Number of LAs supplying performance data may change each year.
(4) Composition of bottom 15% of LAs is subject to change each year.
(5) Trajectories are based on last complete year (2004/05).

**47** Ibid.

**PSA 9b: increase the number of cases in the deregulated private rented sector in receipt of Local Housing Allowance to 740,000 by 2008**

### Measurement

**183.** The baseline for measuring this target is February 2005 when 43,500 cases in the deregulated private rented sector were in receipt of the Local Housing Allowance. In May 2005, there were 44,700 cases across nine Pathfinder areas. Until nationwide rollout of the Local Housing Allowance, progress towards the target will be measured using data covering 100 per cent of the claimants in the existing pilot areas. Once national rollout commences, the target will be monitored and measured using quarterly administrative data on reported performance which are submitted to the Department for Work and Pensions by local authorities.[48] It is not compulsory to return the data, but most local authorities do so.

**184.** Further information can be found in the PSA Technical Note.[49]

### Performance

**185.** Performance against this target is **not yet assessed**. As of November 2005, the number of cases in the deregulated private rented sector in receipt of the local housing allowance was 63,700 across nine Pathfinder areas and nine Second Wave Group pilot areas. The total number of cases in the deregulated private rented sector in receipt of Housing Benefit nationally as at August 2005 was around 729,000.

### Reasons for progress

- The Green Paper *A New Deal for Welfare: Empowering people to work*[50] published in January 2006 contains proposals for a national Local Housing Allowance Scheme in the private rented sector. The Green Paper also sets out several key aspects of the current Local Housing Allowance policy which the Department wishes to modify, to deliver a national scheme that is fair, affordable and that supports its wider welfare reform principles. In particular, consideration is being given to introducing the national Local Housing Allowance scheme for new claims only in the private rented sector.

- As the PSA target requires Local Housing Allowance to have been applied to the entire private sector, this would clearly have implications for the rate of progress towards the target. Subject to the outcome of the consultation exercise on the Green Paper, these implications will be reassessed with HM Treasury.

- The Local Housing Allowance is currently operating in 18 local authorities – nine original Pathfinder areas which began implementation from November 2003 and a further nine Second Wave Group areas which implemented the Local Housing Allowance from April 2005.

**48** Housing Benefit management information quarterly data which is audited internally and published every 3 months at www.dwp.gov.uk/asd/hbctb.asp or a claimant level 100% scan (a new data stream).

**49** www.dwp.gov.uk/publications/dwp/2004/psa/tech_note_2005_2008.pdf

**50** www.dwp.gov.uk/aboutus/welfarereform

- The evaluation of the Local Housing Allowance in the Pathfinder areas is on track and policy issues arising from this are being addressed. The evaluation is due to finish later in 2006, and seven evaluation reports have already been published on the Department's website.[51] Evaluation indicates that Local Housing Allowance has been successful in pathfinder authorities. Ongoing evaluation in Pathfinder areas will inform design of the Local Housing Allowance for the private sector. The Second Wave Group is not subject to the evaluation but is assessed on operational readiness.

51 www.dwp.gov.uk/housingbenefit/lha/evaluation/

**PSA 9c: increase the number of cases in receipt of the Local Housing Allowance where the rent is paid directly to the claimant to 470,000 by 2008**

### Measurement

**186.** The baseline for this target is February 2005 when the number of cases in receipt of the Local Housing Allowance where rent was paid directly to the claimant, was 38,200. In May 2005, there were 38,500 cases. Until nationwide rollout of the Local Housing Allowance, progress towards the target will be measured using data covering 100 per cent of the claimants in the existing pilot areas. Once national rollout commences, the target will be monitored and measured using quarterly administrative data on reported performance which are submitted to the Department by local authorities.[52] It is not compulsory to return the data, but most local authorities do so.

**187.** Further information can be found in the PSA Technical Note.[53]

### Performance

**188.** Performance against this target is **not yet assessed**. As of November 2005 the number of cases in receipt of the local housing allowance where rent was paid directly to the claimant, was 53,800 across nine Pathfinder areas and nine Second Wave Group pilot areas.

### Reasons for progress

**189.** Refer to reasons for progress under PSA 9b.

52 Housing Benefit management information quarterly data which is audited internally and published every 3 months at www.dwp.gov.uk/asd/hbctb.asp or a claimant level 100% scan (a new data stream).

53 www.dwp.gov.uk/publications/dwp/2004/psa/tech_note_2005_2008.pdf

**PSA target 10: Reduce overpayments from fraud and error in Income Support and Jobseeker's Allowance and in Housing Benefit**

**PSA 10a: by 2010, reduce overpayments from fraud and error in Income Support and Jobseeker's Allowance by 15 per cent**

### Measurement

**190.** The present fraud and error measurement system for Income Support (including Income Support for pensioners – now Pension Credit) and Jobseeker's Allowance was developed almost ten years ago. Over that period, the Department's understanding of fraud and error has developed, and there have been a number of changes in the way benefits are administered and paid to customers.

**191.** The Department has taken the opportunity to develop and improve the measurement system. This has led to a methodology for estimating fraud and error significantly different from that used before and it was therefore appropriate to use a new baseline figure for the target set in SR2004, which will be measured using this new methodology. This new baseline figure is due to become available towards the end of 2006. The methodology allows for the effect of these changes on the measure to be estimated.

**192.** To produce estimates of the percentage of benefit overpaid due to fraud and error, data is drawn from randomly selected samples of Income Support and Jobseeker's Allowance cases and results are published twice a year. By its nature, this method is complex, but the National Audit Office (NAO) has approved the Department's methodology and the data are published as National Statistics. It has also been commended by the NAO as being at the forefront of developing estimates of welfare loss in the western world.[54]

**193.** Further information can be found in the PSA Technical Note.[55]

### Performance

**194.** Progress towards this target is **not yet assessed** as the baseline against which performance will be measured has yet to be determined.

**195. SR2002 target rolled forward – PSA 10:** *reduce losses from fraud and error for people of working age – in Income Support and Jobseeker's Allowance, with a 33 per cent reduction by March 2004 and 50 per cent by 2006.*

### SR2002 Performance

**196.** The Department is **on course** to meet this target. Results published as National Statistics in December 2005[56] estimated that fraud and error in Income Support and Jobseeker's Allowance had reduced by 44 per cent by March 2005 from a baseline of 10.4 per cent in 1997–98. Although the reported reduction has been adjusted to account for changes in measurement methodology over time, these adjustments are not reflected in Figure 23. The Department has made good progress in reducing fraud which now stands at its lowest ever level at an estimated 0.8 per cent of benefit expenditure.

54 www.nao.org.uk/publications/nao_reports/02-03/0203393.pdf
55 www.dwp.gov.uk/publications/dwp/2004/psa/tech_note_2005_2008.pdf
56 Fraud and Error in Income Support, Jobseeker's Allowance and Pension Credit from April 2004 to March 2005: Headline Report www.dwp.gov.uk/asd/asd2/fraud.asp

Figure 23 **Levels of fraud, customer and official error compared with the target**

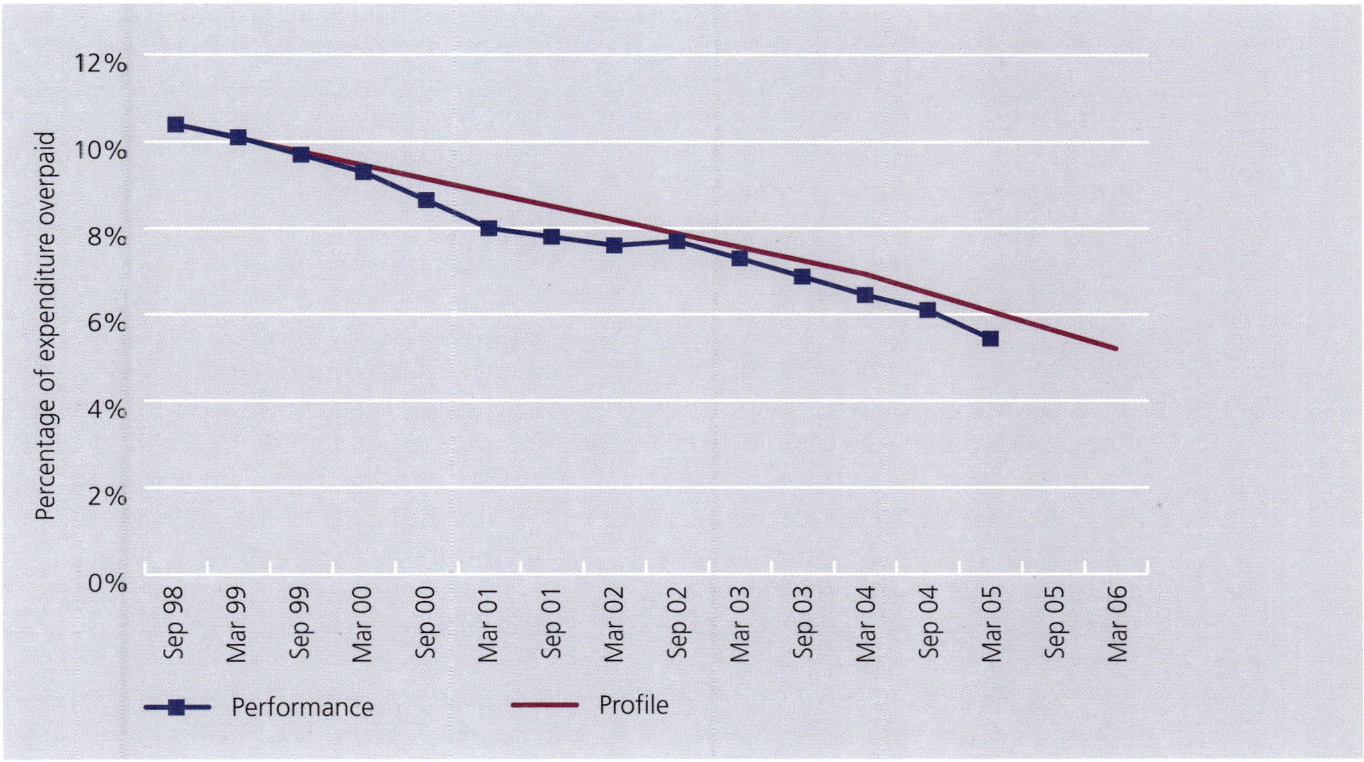


### Reasons for progress

**197.** mproved performance is attributed to:

- Intelligence-led fraud investigation.
- More effective data matching at point of claim and throughout the life of the claim.
- Setting of clear priorities for staff.

**198.** More work is needed to address the level of error in the benefit system. The Department is developing a long-term strategy to tackle this. Work to develop this strategy has commenced and is due to be completed later in 2006. In the short term, an Error Task Force has also been set up with a specific remit to reduce official error.

**The Department has taken the opportunity to develop and improve the measurement system.**

**199.** The Department is moving towards administering benefits from fewer sites which will support greater standardisation of benefit processing, while ensuring that the more difficult claims are handled by the most expert staff. Other plans to bear down on these problems in future focus mainly on better prevention, reducing benefit complexity, inspecting key areas of performance and greater use of data matching.

**200.** Details of what has been achieved on fraud and the Department's future proposals are set out in the strategy paper *Reducing fraud in the benefit system: Achievements and ambitions*[57] published in October 2005. The paper outlines the successful policies that have been developed since 1997 and how increased data matching, new technology and future developments such as the identity card will be used to continue to drive fraud out of the system.

**PSA 10b: by 2008, reduce overpayments from fraud and error in Housing Benefit by 25 per cent.**

## Measurement

**201.** This target will be measured against the 2002–03 baseline when an estimate equivalent to 5.9 per cent of Housing Benefit expenditure was overpaid to customers below state pension age. In January 2006, the baseline estimate was revised downwards from 6.2 per cent due to an improvement in methodology. Further information can be found in the PSA Technical Note[58] and on the Department's website.[59]

**202.** SR 2004 targets were set in summer 2004 when the measurement of fraud and error in Housing Benefit was still relatively new. It was also still too early in the SR2002 reporting cycle to draw firm enough conclusions to justify increasing the target. Consequently, the initial target to reduce overpayments by 25 per cent by March 2006, which was considered quite challenging, was maintained until March 2008.

## Performance

**203.** There has been **slippage** in performance against this target. Estimates for the 12 month period to March 2005 show a 2 per cent increase in Housing Benefit fraud and error compared to the baseline.

57 www.dwp.gov.uk/publications/dwp/2005/fsu/reducingfraud.pdf

58 www.dwp.gov.uk/publications/dwp/2004/psa/tech_note_2005_2008.pdf

59 www.dwp.gov.uk/asd/asd2/fraud_hb/hbmasterjan06.pdf

**204.** Improvements to the methodology used in the Housing Benefit Review have led to the baseline estimate being revised downwards in January 2006. All subsequent estimates of progress have also been revised. These suggest that current progress is no longer in line with previous projections that indicated the Department was likely to exceed the target. Revised projections that take account of latest estimates are not yet complete.

Figure 24 **Reduction in the proportion of Housing Benefit expenditure overpaid**

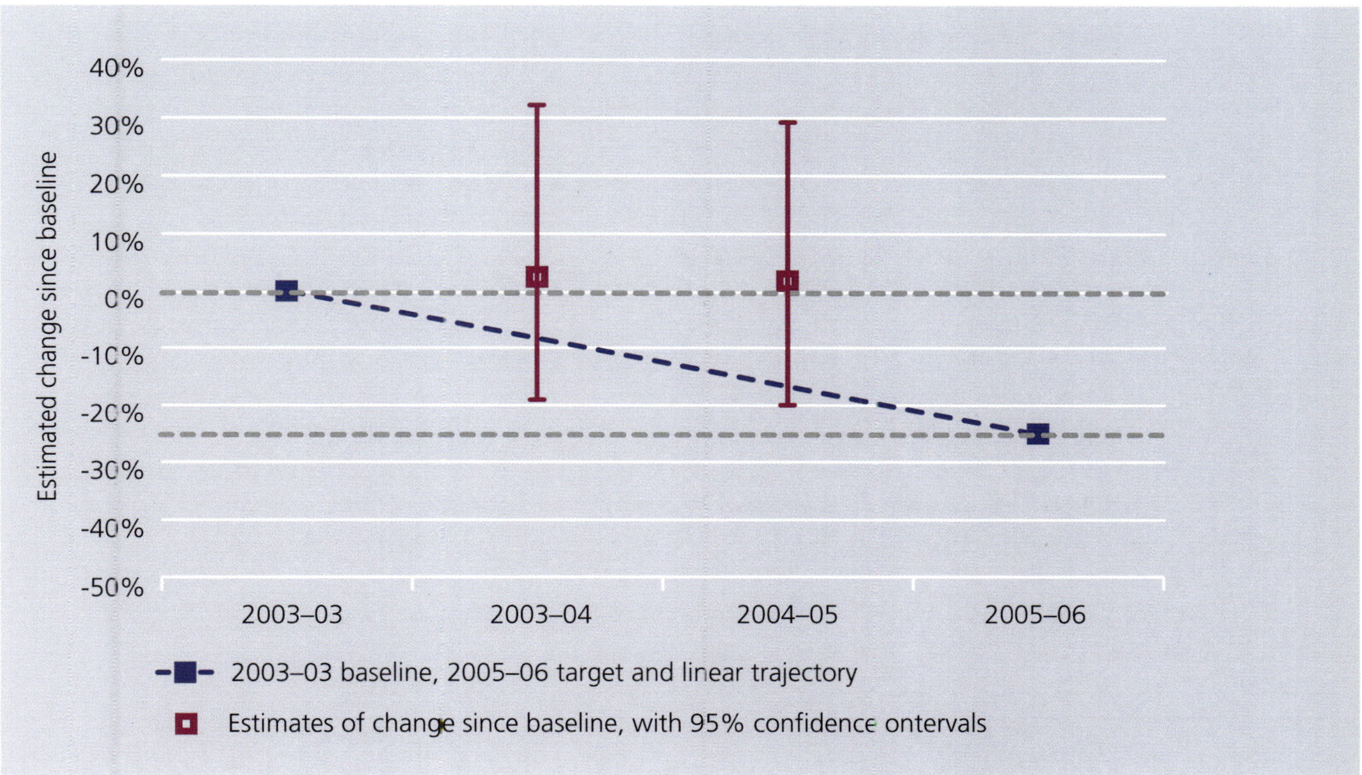


**205.** SR2002 target, rolled forward – PSA 10b: *by spring 2006, reduce losses from fraud and error for people of working age in Housing Benefit by 25 per cent.*

**SR2002 Performance**

**206.** There has been **slippage** against this target. Latest estimates for the 12 month period to March 2005 show a 2 per cent increase in Housing Benefit overpayments. Due to an improvement in methodology, the baseline figure against which progress is measured has been revised downwards to 5.9 per cent.

**207.** Subsequent estimates of past progress have also been revised. As a result the target is more difficult to meet than had previously been thought and slippage has been identified too late to take corrective action.

### Improving performance

**208.** In April 2004 the system of annual renewals for all Housing Benefit claimants was replaced with a risk-based approach to in-claim checks. The Department increased the frequency of Housing Benefit data matches and introduced a new risk-scoring service to support local authorities with the changeover. However the Department recognised that it would take time for local authorities to fully adjust to the new system. Therefore progress was expected to be slow until 2005–06. In 2005–06 the volume of in-claim checks that authorities are expected to undertake has been increased and a stricter monitoring regime has been introduced. These factors should become apparent in the Housing Benefit Review publication covering 2005–06.

**209.** Some early progress had been expected before 2005–06 due to improvements in counter-fraud activity. Prior to the revision of methodology in January 2006, progress appeared to be in line with these expectations. However the latest estimates indicate that this early progress has not been achieved. It also appears that the deterrent impact of increases in local authority sanctions has not been as great as anticipated.

**210.** The Department has identified that the main cause of Housing Benefit overpayments is failure on the part of claimants to report changes promptly. The latest evidence suggests that increasing the volume of sanctions does not address this problem adequately. Therefore, the Department is undertaking a programme of research and analysis in order to develop a more effective strategy for tackling claimant error. However the results of this strategy will not feed through until after 2005–06 and will therefore have no impact on the SR2002 target.

**The Department has identified that the main cause of Housing Benefit overpayments is failure on the part of claimants to report changes promptly.**

# PART SIX **EFFICIENCY AND OUTSTANDING TARGETS FROM PREVIOUS SPENDING REVIEWS**

## The Efficiency Challenge

Delivery of PSA targets is set in the context of the Government's efficiency agenda, which forms part of the Spending Review settlement.

The Department is required to achieve a reduction in the size of its workforce of 40,000 posts with redeployment of 10,000 posts to frontline roles and deliver annual savings of at least £960 million by 2007–08 while, at the same time, maintaining and improving customer services.

In conjunction with this, the Department has also been set a target by the Lyons review[60] to relocate 4,000 posts away from London and the South East to other regions by March 2008.

More detailed information about the Department's efficiency targets and their measurement can be found in the Efficiency Technical Note.[61]

**The Department is required to achieve a reduction in the size of its workforce of 40,000 posts.**

**60** www.hm-treasury.gov.uk/consultations_and_legislation/lyons/consult_lyons_index.cfm#final
**61** www.dwp.gov.uk/aboutus/efficiency_tech_note.pdf

**211.** The Department will need to meet its PSA targets and deliver its wider objectives while achieving the efficiency challenge that was set by the Government as part of the 2004 Spending Review settlement. The efficiency targets and progress towards the achievement of those targets are summarised in Figure 25 below.

Figure 25 **Progress against the efficiency targets**

| Efficiency Challenge | Departmental target for March 2008 | Achievement December 2005 |
|---|---|---|
| Annual financial savings | £960 million | £602 million[62], of which £313 million relates to 2004–05. The total is split between £316 million cashable (expenditure-reducing) savings and £286 million non-cashable (cost-avoidance) savings. |
| Net headcount reduction | 30,000 | 14,860 |
| Posts to be redeployed to customer-facing roles | 10,000 | 5,594 |
| Posts to be relocated from London and the South East | 4,000 | 3,176 |

**212.** The Department is on course to achieve all the efficiency targets and the annual financial savings have already been built into its budget. Despite the progress to date, this continues to be an extremely challenging agenda, particularly maintaining overall performance and customer service while reducing the Department's headcount substantially.

**213.** The Department is working to achieve its efficiency targets through a combination of streamlining overheads, improving business processes supported by better IT, driving up performance to that of the current best, and more efficient procurement.

**214.** Following the creation of Jobcentre Plus and The Pension Service, the former Jobcentre and social security office networks are being rationalised and new contact centres have been introduced, standardising customer contact and processing work, and enabling the Department to achieve economies of scale. These efficiencies will mean that the Department needs fewer staff to continue to deliver a high level of service to customers.

62 This figure is higher than the figure of around £300 million published in Budget 2006, as a result of the completion of a comprehensive review to validate efficiency savings.

**215.** Alongside the business transformations the Department aims to achieve substantial savings through the completed re-alignment of its IT supplier contracts; and through the release of estate, as workforce and office numbers reduce. Among the measures the Department is taking are:

- a comprehensive transformation of The Pension Service;
- the creation of the modern Disability and Carers Service with a headcount 22 per cent less by March 2008;
- continued rollout of Jobcentre Plus and the reform of benefit processing;
- a review of the child support service;
- further modernisation of policy-making processes and corporate support functions; and
- direct payment of benefits and pensions.

## Progress

**216.** The Department has invested around £2.8 billion over the last two spending reviews in modern IT infrastructure that has given it the opportunity to operate more efficiently and the ability to release more staff for frontline work.

**217.** Substantial progress has continued to be made over the past year in reducing the Department's workforce. Since March 2004 the workforce has reduced by over 14,000 and over 3,000 posts have been relocated from London and the South East Over 5,500 posts have been redeployed to customer-facing roles in Jobcentre Plus.

**218.** Progress made in the delivery of efficiency savings in the Department for Work and Pensions and five other departments was examined by the National Audit Office in the summer of 2005 with the report *Progress in Improving Government Efficiency*[63] published in February 2006. For this Department, there was positive recognition of the progress made through work on direct payment, integrated resource management, HR modernisation and estates rationalisation. The Department was also commended for its governance and development of measurement methodology to ensure that savings achieved represent efficiency and not cuts by preserving and improving services for customers.

**219.** The Department has been developing and refining the plans for meeting the remainder of the efficiency challenge. Information about the overall shape of these plans, and how businesses are being transformed over the next two years to deliver the efficiency challenge, can be found throughout this report. The Department is also committed to regular reports of progress through future Departmental and Autumn Performance Reports, and through the business plans and annual reports and accounts of each of its executive agencies.

## Quality measures

**220.** The efficiency target will be met if the overall efficiency savings, including the staff savings, are achieved without detriment to performance across all areas of the Department's activity and customers experience no diminution in the service they receive. Performance measurement will be based on the methodology developed by the

**63** www.nao.org.uk/publications/nao_reports/05-06/0506802i.pdf

Department and the Office for National Statistics for the Atkinson Review of the Measurement of Government Output and Productivity, and will be consistent with the recommendations in chapter 11 of the Review's final report.[64]

**221.** Under this methodology efficiency is a measure of how well the organisation uses its inputs to produce its outputs. Inputs are all the resources used by the Department to produce goods and services, and will be measured in financial terms. The Department's outputs will be measured by a cost-weighted index, where the unit cost of production is used as a proxy for the value of the output. In line with Atkinson recommendations, outputs will be adjusted for quality where possible.

**222.** These measures will be supplemented by other information which the Department monitors and publishes on a regular basis in, for example, forward plans and performance reports, which will help to provide a rounded picture of the Department's performance. Additional performance information includes progress towards the Department's PSA targets and agency targets for business delivery and customer service which are set annually and published in agency Business Plans.

**223.** There will also be a continuation of the monitoring of service through 'mystery shopping' (tests of services performed by independent organisations replicating customer experience), surveys of customer perceptions and reviewing feedback received in other ways, for example from voluntary and advisory bodies.

## 2002 Spending Review targets not rolled forward

**PSA target 8: Make significant progress towards modernising welfare delivery so that by 2005, 85 per cent of customers have their benefit paid into their bank accounts.**

### Performance

**224.** Final assessment: this target was **met early**.

**225.** The base year for this target was 2002 when 43 per cent of customers were paid by Direct Payment and by April 2005 nearly 97 per cent of all benefit accounts were being paid by Direct Payment. Latest figures for December 2005, the target end date, show that this has remained stable and over 97 per cent are still being paid directly into a bank account.

### Reasons for progress

**226.** In order to achieve these continued benefits, and realise further savings, targets for new claims and live load on Direct Payment were agreed in respect of all customer groups for 2005–06. Targets have formed a critical part of achieving the success to date and are likely to continue to be required in future years to ensure that the savings are not eroded.

64 www.statistics.gov.uk/about/data/methodology/specific/PublicSector/atkinson/downloads/Atkinson_cha11.pdf

**PSA target 9:** Improve the delivery of the Department's services by setting annual published targets for each major business, addressing accuracy, unit costs and customer service, becoming progressively more demanding over the three-year period.

**227.** This target applies to the Department's three major executive agencies, The Pension Service, the Child Support Agency and Jobcentre Plus. In order to provide a wider perspective on the Department's progress in this area, this report also includes the Disability and Carers Service, which became an executive agency in November 2004, although this is not a requirement of the SR2002 PSA target. Outturn performance assessments for the 2004–05 targets were published in the Autumn Performance Report 2005.[65]

**228.** The target levels for 2005–06 are set out below. Validated outturn data for 2005–06 will be reported in each agency's annual report and accounts in July 2006, and final performance assessments will be published in the 2006 Autumn Performance Report.

## PSA 9a: The Pension Service

Figure 26 **2005–06 targets for The Pension Service**

| | Targets for 2005–06 |
|---|---|
| Accuracy | Achieve a Pension Credit accuracy rate of 96 per cent. |
| | Achieve a State Pension claims accuracy rate of 98 per cent. |
| Customer service | Ensure that 92 per cent of telephone calls to The Pension Service centres are answered by customer advisers. |
| | Ensure that less than 1 per cent of attempted calls receive the engaged tone or message. |
| Unit costs | Achieve a unit cost target of £25.50 |

65 www.dwp.gov.uk/publications/dwp/2005/autumnreport/

### PSA 9b: Child Support Agency

**229.** The performance targets for 2004-05 were rolled forward to 2005-06, with the exception of the debt target, which was introduced for 2005-06.

Figure 27 **2005–06 targets for the Child Support Agency**

| Targets for 2005–06 | |
|---|---|
| Accuracy | By 31 March 2006, accuracy on the last decision made for all maintenance calculations checked in the year to be correct to the nearest penny in at least 90 per cent of cases. |
| Case compliance | By 31 March 2006 to be collecting child maintenance and/or arrears from 78 per cent of all cases with a maintenance liability using the collection service. |
| Cash compliance | By 31 March 2006 to be collecting at least 75 per cent of child maintenance and/or arrears due to be paid through the collection service. |
| Debt (new target introduced for 2005–06) | To collect arrears equivalent to 30 per cent of the amount accruing (as a result of non-payment of regular maintenance) between 1 April 2005 and 31 March 2006. |
| Unit costs | Achieve a cost per case of £202. |

### PSA 9c: Jobcentre Plus

Figure 28 **2005–06 targets for Jobcentre Plus**

| Targets for 2005–06 | | |
|---|---|---|
| Accuracy | Income Support | 90 per cent |
| | Jobseeker's Allowance | 90 per cent |
| Achieve an 81 per cent customer service level in the delivery of the standards set out in the Customers' and Employers' Charters. | | |
| Unit cost for each benefit processed | | £28.24 |
| Unit cost for each job entry outcome point achieved. | | £217.03 |

## Disability and Carers Service[66]

Figure 29 **2005–06 target for the Disability and Carers Service**

| Performance area | 2005–06 target | |
|---|---|---|
| Accuracy of decision making and payment | | |
| Disability Living Allowance/ Attendance Allowance | 90 per cent | |
| Carer's Allowance | 96 per cent | |
| Customer service: Average actual clearance time for new claims (days) | | |
| Disability Living Allowance | New claims | 39 |
| | Reconsiderations | 35 |
| | Appeals | 37 |
| Attendance Allowance | New claims | 22 |
| | Reconsiderations | 35 |
| | Appeals | 35 |
| Carer's Allowance | New claims | 22 |
| | Appeals | 35 |
| Customer service: Telephony – new target from 2005-06. Ensure that 90 per cent of calls to the national Helpline are answered, and that less than 1 per cent of calls are blocked or receive an engaged tone. | | |
| Unit costs | £131.56 | |

**66** Not part of PSA target, but included as additional information.

## Ongoing target from the 1998 Comprehensive Spending Review

Promote policies consistent with a change in the ratio of spending on pensions by the State to spending on pensions by the private sector from around 60:40 to 50:50 by 2025 and to 40:60 in 2050

### Measurement

**230.** The definition is the ratio of total state pension income to private pension income of all benefit units in Great Britain over State Pension age (defined as single people over State Pension age or couples where the man is over State Pension age).

**231.** The data comes from the Pensioners' Income Series – National Statistics published annually by the Department, based on the Family Resources Survey. The latest data relates to 2004–05.[67]

### Performance

**232.** This target is **ongoing**.[68] The mix of state and private income in 2050 will be affected by any policy changes following on from the Pension Commission's report in November 2005, the National Pensions Debate and the pension reform White Paper. These major uncertainties mean it is not yet possible to forecast the spending mix in 2050 with any confidence.

**233.** The ratio of state to private spending has not changed significantly – it has fallen from 57:43 in 1996–97 to 56:44 in 2004–05, the latest year available. As the original aspiration to reverse the ratio was a very long-term one, and as by their nature policies to increase private pension provision will not impact on pensioners' incomes for many years, the lack of significant change is not a surprise.

### Reasons for progress

**234.** Since the target was set, State Pension spending on current pensioners has become more generous, especially that for lower income pensioners, with the immediate impact of making the target harder to achieve.

**235.** Since 1997, measures like the introduction of Pension Credit, the State Second Pension's more generous treatment of carers and disabled persons, higher-than-average real increases in the Basic State Pension and universal payments like Winter Fuel Payments have resulted in over 2 million pensioners being lifted out of absolute low income.

**236.** Policies have also been introduced that should increase private pension spending – such as the introduction of stakeholder pensions, the Pension Protection Fund, the new Pensions Regulator and Informed Choice programme – but these will take years, if not decades, to feed through.

**237.** Occupational pension income and income from personal pensions has grown faster than benefit income during recent years. This has determined the development of the ratio as set out in the PSA target. However it should be noted that if earnings and other income were included in the target the ratio of state to private spending would already be only

67 www.dwp.gov.uk/asd/asd6/pensioners_income.asp

68 This non-standard performance rating reflects the long-term nature of this target.

50:50 in 2004–05. This ratio has been on a gradually improving trend, down from 53:47 in 1996–97, partly on the back of the increasing trend of people working beyond state pension age. If the target were to include all sources of private income, such as earnings and other income, and if the real growth rates seen in all the sources of pensioner income in the decade to 2004–05 persist over the coming decades, the ratio of public to private would turn 40:60 around 2050.

**238.** People are also increasingly diversifying their saving behaviour, and retirees now hold large amounts of housing equity and other assets, which they may use to generate further private source income in future. As presently constituted, the target fails to capture this.

**Occupational pension income and income from personal pensions, has grown faster than benefit income during recent years.**

# 04 THE DEPARTMENT'S AGENCIES

THIS CHAPTER PROVIDES INFORMATION ABOUT THE AIMS AND ACTIVITIES OF THE DEPARTMENT FOR WORK AND PENSIONS' EXECUTIVE AGENCIES. ADDITIONAL INFORMATION CAN BE FOUND IN EACH AGENCY'S BUSINESS PLAN AND ANNUAL REPORT AND ACCOUNTS, AND ON THE FOLLOWING WEBSITES:

www.jobcentreplus.gov.uk

www.thepensionservice.gov.uk

www.csa.gov.uk

www.appeals-service.gov.uk

www.therentservice.gov.uk

www.hse.gov.uk

239. Validated performance data for 2005–06 for each agency will be published in their Annual Report and Accounts later in 2006.

## Jobcentre Plus

### Introduction

240. Jobcentre Plus provides support to people seeking to enter or return to work and administers a range of benefits to those unable to work.

241. Jobcentre Plus is also playing a central role in the modernisation of welfare delivery and is engaged in a programme of major change. In 2005–06 a comprehensive review of management and support structures has been completed and the process of centralising benefit payments into centres of excellence has begun.

### Purpose

242. Jobcentre Plus' purpose is to provide work for those who can and support for those who cannot, by:

- helping disadvantaged people into work, as a route out of poverty;
- providing financial support as a safety net for people while they are out of work;
- addressing inequalities of opportunity;
- protecting the integrity of the benefit system; and
- working with employers and partners to address market failure in the labour market.

## Delivery Strategy

243. The Jobcentre Plus 2005–06 Business Plan[69] was published in March 2005, setting out the priorities for the year:

- transforming for customers;
- delivering performance;
- delivering services more efficiently and effectively; and
- delivering the Values through its people.

## Key activities in 2005–06

### Transforming for customers

244. Jobcentre Plus has:

- rolled out over 700 new integrated offices;
- expanded Pathways to Work for Incapacity Benefit customers to 14 more Jobcentre Plus districts and placed over 17,000 customers into work;
- introduced Employer Direct online;
- enhanced the Internet Job Bank to allow employers to input their vacancies directly;
- progressed plans to centralise benefit processing;
- restructured the contact centre network and introduced a new contact management system; and
- paid benefit for more people straight into their bank account.

### Delivering performance

245. Jobcentre Plus' 2004–05 targets and outturn performance were reported in the Agency's 2004-05 Annual Report and Accounts published in October 2005.[70] Performance targets for 2005–06 were published in the Business Plan in March 2005.[71]

### Delivering services more efficiently and effectively

246. Jobcentre Plus has:

- implemented the first stage of the Organisation Design Review, a process to re-structure and streamline the organisation, and reduced the number of districts from 83 to 50;
- reduced staffing from 74,913 in April 2005 to 71,222 at the end of March 2005, meeting its target;
- introduced components of the Standard Operating Model that will ensure consistent and efficient processes;
- reviewed its contracts with providers;

**Jobcentre Plus' purpose is to provide work for those who can and support for those who cannot.**

69 www.jobcentreplus.gov.uk/JCP/static/Dev_008277.pdf

70 www.jobcentreplus.gov.uk/JCP/Aboutus/Publications/Annual_Report_2004_-_05/index.html

71 www.jobcentreplus.gov.uk/JCP/static/Dev_008277.pdf

- introduced the online 'Job Warehouse' which currently hosts 50 per cent of the total vacancy stock available to customers;
- rolled out Employer Direct online nationally; and
- implemented the New Deal for Skills with the Learning and Skills Council.

### Delivering the Values through its people

**247.** Jobcentre Plus has:

- revised the skills of managers through the Pathways to Leadership training programme;
- started to roll out the Jobcentre Plus Working Together programme; and
- made effective use of TalkDirect, a programme that gives staff access to members of the Jobcentre Plus Board and local senior managers.

## The Pension Service

**248.** The objectives of The Pension Service for 2005–06 were:

- to combat poverty among today's pensioners;
- to encourage future pensioners to save for their retirement through the private sector, and to provide security for those likely to rely on state provision;
- to further improve and modernise services for today's and future pensioners; and
- for its staff, high levels of job satisfaction – based on continuous learning and achievement.

### Delivery strategy

**249.** The Pension Service 2005–06 Business Plan[72], published in March 2005 set out:

- the service customers could expect when contacting The Pension Service about any element of their retirement;
- the performance standards to be achieved within the year; and
- the planned distribution of resources.

72 www.thepensionservice.gov.uk/pdf/busplan/tpsbusplan0506.pdf

## Key activities in 2005–06

### Pension Credit

**250.** The implementation of Pension Credit has been a key priority for The Pension Service. Around 2.7 million households receive Pension Credit, in comparison to 1.8 million households who received its predecessor, the Minimum Income Guarantee. The Pension Service has a PSA target of paying Pension Credit to at least 3.2 million households by 2008.

### Pension forecasts

**251.** The Pension Service continues to deliver its forecasting service to over 12 million future pensioners, responding to requests for Individual Pension Forecasts and issuing Combined Pension Forecasts. The Pension Service also issues Automatic Pension Forecasts to people who have not received a Combined Pension Forecast or Individual Pension Forecast within the previous 12 months. Details of current performance can be found in Chapter Three, in the report on PSA 7.

**252.** Real-Time Pension Forecasts were launched on 25 October 2004. This is an online service in which customers can contact the Department electronically to obtain a State Pension Forecast. Because of the need to protect personal information, customers have to first register with the Government Gateway. Between the launch of the service in October 2004 and the end of March 2006 over 107,000 Real-Time Pension Forecasts have been requested.

### Local Service

**253.** During 2005–06, The Pension Service continued to work towards delivering Local Service as part of an integrated service developed jointly with its partners, national and local, statutory and voluntary, and built around the needs of older people.

**254.** The Pension Service Local Service is developing Joint Teams with local community partners. These teams have provided an opportunity to capture a much wider customer base and reach some of the most vulnerable pensioners. They have had a significant impact on take-up of both departmental benefits and local authority services.

**255.** Since September 2005 existing Pension Credit customers have been contacted and invited to claim Council Tax Benefit and/or Housing Benefit. Since December 2005, customers who contact the Pension Credit Application Line to make an application for Pension Credit have also been able to claim Housing Benefit and Council Tax Benefit during the one phone call.

**256.** Mystery shopping will continue to be used to assess the quality of service to customers. The programme will be designed to measure the key elements of service that customers said were important in the most recent national customer survey.

**Customers are now able to make their claim to State Pension in one phone call.**

### The Pension Transformation Programme

**257.** The Pension Transformation Programme is an ambitious programme that will result in the transformation of The Pension Service business, organisation and supporting systems. This reform, to be phased in over the coming years, will support the Government's commitment to the delivery of efficient, high-quality public services. It will deliver a Pension Service that:

- increases take-up of entitlements, to reduce poverty;
- improves customer service; and
- improves efficiency.

**258.** In 2005, The Pension Service began to transform the State Pension application process by providing a modernised telephony-enabled service that is faster and simpler. Customers are now able to make their claim to State Pension in one phone call, at the end of which they know their entitlement and when they will receive their payments. These new services began in August 2005 in Newcastle Pension Centre, which serves London customers and was extended in November 2005 in Dundee and Swansea Pension Centres.

## Child Support Agency

**259.** The Agency's purpose is to ensure that parents who live apart from their children contribute financially to their upkeep.

### Delivery strategy

**260.** The Child Support Agency published its 2005–06 Business Plan[73] in March 2005, setting out the challenges the Agency faced in delivering its service to clients. The Agency's priority during 2005–06 was to deliver a good level of service to its clients, while focusing on supporting staff by ensuring that they had the right tools, and recognising development and knowledge; and working with Electronic Data Systems (EDS) to continue to improve the computer system and improve business performance.

**261.** In February 2006 the Agency published its Operational Improvement Plan[74] setting out a programme for the next three years to deliver more money for more children. The plan focuses on four main elements:

- getting it right: gathering information and assessing applications;
- keeping it right: active case management;
- putting it right: enforcing responsibilities; and
- getting the best from the organisation.

**262.** In each element the plan sets out the issues, the action being taken to address them, and the results the Agency's clients can expect.

**73** www.csa.gov.uk
**74** www.csa.gov.uk/pdf/english/reports/oip.pdf

## Key activities in 2005-06

263. The Agency's business plan outlined six main priorities for 2005–06. These were to:

- **Improve the position for new scheme clients and maintain the position for old scheme clients.** Having improved in many areas since April 2004, the Agency's performance is currently stable. This provides the Agency with a solid foundation on which to deliver future improvements.

  Significant progress has been made on improving the management information available to the Department in respect of both old and new schemes, resulting in publication of the CSA's Quarterly Summary Statistics.[75]

  Significant improvements were made in the telephony service during 2005-06, with the Agency answering 91 per cent of calls available in staff queues compared to 84 per cent in 2004–05. During the same period, the average waiting time for a call to be answered improved by 1 minute 32 seconds for new scheme and 22 seconds for old scheme cases.

- **Continue to improve effectiveness of enforcement.** The creation of the Enforcement Directorate has increased the Agency's focus and activities in this important area. The Enforcement Teams are becoming much more successful in utilising their enforcement powers and this is demonstrated by the significant improvement in the in-month cash collections achieved, rising from £0.52 million in January 2005 to £1.44 million in March 2006.

- **Support staff.** Given the highly stressful and sensitive nature of their work, Child Support Agency staff have one of the hardest jobs in Government. Improved attendance management procedures have gone some way to improve conditions, and attendance management figures have improved from an average of 15.9 days lost per person in 2004–05, to 12 days in 2005–06.

- **Prepare to move existing cases to the new arrangements (migration and conversion).** The CSA Operational Improvement Plan sets out how the Agency will stabilise and improve performance over a three year period. Ministers have always said that no decision will be taken on when to convert old scheme cases until they are confident that the new scheme is working well. In February 2006, the Secretary of State commissioned Sir David Henshaw to undertake a fundamental redesign of child support policy and delivery mechanisms.

- **Continue to improve Corporate Governance.** Throughout the year the Agency has continued to work closely with the Department's Risk and Assurance Division to identify and improve governance processes.

Having improved in many areas since April 2004, the Agency's performance is currently stable.

75 www.dwp.gov.uk/asd/csa.asp

## Disability and Carers Service

**264.** The Disability and Carers Service became an Executive Agency of the Department for Work and Pensions in November 2004.

**265.** The agency's objective is to enable independence by supporting the diverse needs of disabled people and carers. It aims to achieve this by treating its customers with respect and providing an accessible, accurate and efficient service.

### Delivery strategy

**266.** Plans for the Disability and Carers Service were included in the Disability and Carers Service Business Plan published in March 2005.[76] In 2005–06 the delivery strategy was to:

- know what customers want;
- work with others to serve shared customers;
- increase the capability of staff;
- simplify business processes;
- invest in and improve infrastructure;
- ensure customers receive their correct entitlement at the right time;
- increase the share of resources in customer-related activities; and
- measure and report progress honestly.

### Key activities in 2005–06

**267.** The Disability and Carers Service embarked on a major programme of transformation to improve the efficiency of its service to ensure customers' needs are at the heart of the business and improve the experience of staff and relationships with stakeholders.

**268.** The Disability and Carers Service has:

- met all business targets for DLA/AA/CA claims delivery within agreed clearance time and funding;
- significantly improved performance of the DLA/AA national telephone service and achieved Call Centre Association Standards Council accreditation;
- developed and tested a new Decision Making process for DLA including new claim pack, new medical guidance, new training and an IT platform;
- developed proposals for an accredited system for Decision-Makers and their line managers and appointed Chester University as the accreditation partner;
- developed the People Strategy to enable the creation over time of a more flexible, professional, better-supported workforce;
- successfully managed the transfer of work and the redeployment of staff at Sutton Disability Centre which closed in December 2005;
- published the Customer Promise;
- reduced significantly the number of working days lost through staff absence; and
- met its target to reduce overall staff numbers by 300 full-time equivalents by March 2006.

76 www.dwp.gov.uk/publications/dwp/2005/dcd/business_plan06.pdf

## Appeals Service

**269.** The Appeals Service has a clear purpose statement that describes what it seeks to do:

- To bring together the parties to the appeal and the judiciary with all appropriate resources for the fair and independent delivery of decisions in a way that best meets both the expectations of all parties to the appeal and the demands of the public purse.

**270.** In order to achieve this, the Agency aims to continuously improve its service, for example by:

- listening to appellants via independent research into their needs and concerns followed by targeted actions aimed at improving its service;
- working with the President and judiciary to review and improve the service provided to them and the Tribunal;
- working with other Department for Work and Pensions' agencies to ensure the overall service to appellants is as good as it can be; and
- planning for the transfer to the Department for Constitutional Affairs, where it will become part of the Tribunals Service.

### Delivery strategy

**271.** The Appeals Service published its 2005–06 Business Plan in March 2005[77], identifying the Agency's six strategic intents:

- significant improvement in the service to appellants;
- better service to the President and judiciary;
- delivery of an efficient service that provides value for money;
- continuous development of its people, processes and technology to support its modernisation aims;
- contribution to the wider activity of the Department for Work and Pensions in support of its key objectives; and
- working with colleagues in the Department, the Department for Constitutional Affairs and other tribunals, to make a significant contribution to the successful creation of the Tribunals Service.

**2005–06 has been a transition year for The Appeals Service, consolidating and building on progress in recent years.**

77 www.appeals-service.gov.uk/publications/reports_and_business_plan.htm#business_plan

### Key activities in 2005–06

272. 2005–06 has been a transition year for The Appeals Service, consolidating and building on progress in recent years, while undertaking the preparatory work for transfer to the Department of Constitutional Affairs in April 2006.

273. In addition service to appellants has been enhanced by a number of new initiatives, specifically:

- the re-design and re-launch of the Appeals Service website in order to make it a more powerful and effective communication tool; and
- working with other Department for Work and Pensions' agencies to improve the quality of initial decision-making and thereby seek to reduce the overall volume of appeals.

## The Rent Service

274. The Rent Service aims to be 'England's leading provider of impartial, professional, rental valuation services that are fair to customers and other stakeholders'.

275. This contributes to the Department's main Housing Benefit objective which is to ensure customers receive a high quality service, including high levels of accuracy; and to the Office of the Deputy Prime Minister's strategic housing priority which is to ensure that people have decent places to live by improving the sustainability of local environments and neighbourhoods, reviving brown field land, and improving the quality of housing.

276. Key performance targets are set by the Secretary of State following consultation with The Rent Service's main customers and stakeholders and are centred around:

- the quality of determinations and valuations;
- customer satisfaction;
- value for money; and
- speed of processing.

### Delivery Strategy

277. The Rent Service's delivery strategy is to:

- work in close partnership with customers and stakeholders to deliver business priorities;

- ensure that services are provided as efficiently and as cost effectively as possible and that the size of the estate is kept under review to ensure that office space is consistent with business needs;
- continue to deliver a customer-focused service that provides greater access and flexibility to customers and stakeholders by undertaking various surveys to identify areas for further improvements;
- take advantage of new technology, including continuing to invest in IT systems and building on the advances made to date, in order to speed up and improve the quality of overall service delivery; and
- continue to invest in the learning and development of staff and to ensure that they are appropriately rewarded for their performance.

278. The Rent Service's key business priorities for the year can be found in its 2005–06 Business Plan[78] which was published in March 2005.

### Key activities in 2005–06

279. 2005–06 has been an extremely challenging year for The Rent Service. While its main business priority for the year remains achieving its increasingly stretching key performance targets, it has also continued to support the Housing Benefit reforms.

280. These reforms have been implemented in seven new local authorities during 2005–06 and The Rent Service's role, as with the existing Pathfinder authorities, will be to determine the Broad Rental Market Areas within these authorities and to set the Local Housing Allowances.

281. The other main business priorities for the year were to:

- continue to improve the quality of service to customers, including reviewing the customer service framework and strategy;
- further rationalise the size of the estate. The number of operational offices reduced from 33 to 26[79] during 2005–06;
- undertake a series of efficiency reviews of back office functions in order to determine whether the function is still necessary; identify alternative ways of providing the support service and to reduce costs/resources needed to provide the service;
- consolidate IT systems and, in particular, the network infrastructure to improve the management of traffic through the wide area network and thus the speed of overall service delivery;
- develop The Rent Service website and web-based applications;

78 www.therentservice.gov.uk/documents/corporate_publications/business_plan_2005-06.pdf

79 Initial plans were for the number of offices to reduce from 33 to 28 during 2005–06. However, a decision was later taken to close two additional offices during the same period.

- invest the equivalent of 3.7 per cent of direct staff costs in the learning and development of staff; and to ensure that staff continue to develop transferable skills, including attaining professional and vocational qualifications;
- maintain good progress made in reducing sickness absence levels; and
- work with staff's Trade Union representatives through the changes affecting The Rent Service's staff.

## Health and Safety Commission/Executive

**282.** The Health and Safety at Work etc Act 1974 established the Health and Safety Commission (HSC) and the Health and Safety Executive (HSE). HSC and HSE are statutory Non-Departmental Public Bodies, performing their functions on behalf of the Crown. Responsibility for HSC and HSE transferred to the Department for Work and Pensions in July 2002.

**283.** The Health and Safety Commission's primary function is to make arrangements to secure the health, safety and welfare of people at work and the general public. This includes proposing new laws and standards, conducting research and providing information and advice. The Commission reports to the Secretary of State for Work and Pensions, and to other Secretaries of State.

**284.** The Health and Safety Executive advises and assists the Commission in its functions. Together with local authorities, HSE has day-to-day responsibility for enforcing health and safety law, investigating accidents, licensing and approving standards in particularly hazardous areas and commissioning research. HSE has around 4,000 staff, including inspectors, policy advisers, technologists and scientific and medical experts.

**285.** HSC/E's **vision** is to gain recognition of health and safety as a cornerstone of a civilised society and, with that, to achieve a record of workplace health and safety that leads the world.

**286.** HSC/E's **mission** is, working with local authorities, to protect people's health and safety by ensuring that risks in the changing workplace are properly controlled.

### Delivery strategy

**287.** In February 2004, the Health and Safety Commission launched its *Strategy for workplace health and safety in Great Britain to 2010 and beyond*.[80] The Strategy contains four high level themes:

- developing closer partnerships;
- helping people to benefit from effective health and safety management and a sensible health and safety culture;
- focusing on core business by being clear about priorities; and
- communicating the vision.

80 www.hse.gov.uk/aboutus/hsc/strategy.htm

**288.** HSE has set up Strategic Programmes as the main agent for implementing HSC's Strategy and delivering the PSA. There are two Strategic Delivery Programmes (SDPs):

- Fit for work, Fit for life, Fit for Tomorrow (Fit3): designed to deliver the conventional health and safety sub-targets; and
- Major Hazards: regulating and assuring safe management of those industries where failure to manage risks can have catastrophic effects.

**289.** Four Strategic Enabling Programmes support the work of the SDPs, focusing on business involvement, worker involvement, local authorities and enforcement.

### Key activities in 2005-06

- Securing compliance with the law by providing advice and guidance, inspecting workplaces, investigating accidents and complaints and taking enforcement action where necessary.
- Ensuring appropriate risk control measures are in place for major hazard precursor incidents that have the potential to develop into a catastrophic accident.
- Launching *Health Work and Well-being*[81], a new joint strategy with the Department for Work and Pensions and the Department of Health, focused on improving the health and well-being of working age people.
- Setting up the Ministerial Task Force, which aims to provide the impetus to change public sector management culture and has produced a review of sickness absence.
- Using communication to support operational activities. HSE ran major campaigns targeting back pain[82] and slipping and tripping accidents.[83]
- Working with businesses to help them manage work-related stress more effectively. HSE has developed and launched stress management standards.
- Establishing Workplace Health Connect[84]; a service for small firms, providing free and impartial advice on health and safety at work.
- Targeting slips, trips and falls during the final stages of construction projects across the country, with the Fit Out Phase campaign.
- Introducing workplace transport management standards on all aspects of driver training and working to gain stakeholder support.
- Launching practical online tools (CHaSPI and the SME indicator[85]) to help businesses manage their heath and safety more effectively.

81 www.dwp.gov.uk/publications/dwp/2005/health_and_wellbeing.pdf

82 www.hse.gov.uk/msd/backs/
83 www.hse.gov.uk/watchyourstep/
84 www.hse.gov.uk/workplacehealth/
85 The Corporate Health and Safety Performance Index (www.chaspi.info-exchange.com/) and the Small and Medium-sized Enterprise indicator (www.hspi.info-exchange.com/)

- Producing an enforcement communications strategy to position HSE as a firm but fair regulator and use the publicity arising from enforcement to spread health and safety messages
- Launching a website, to support worker involvement in improving health and safety outcomes, along with complementary guidance and case studies for employers.
- Setting up a framework for improved communication and partnership working with our local authority enforcement partners.
- Applying science, research and technology to support delivery of HSC/E's vision, mission and the PSA.

**Health and Safety Sponsorship Unit**

**290.** As HSC/E's sponsor, the Department for Work and Pensions and its Ministers have a number of statutory and non-statutory roles. These include appointing the Commission, approving the Commission's plan of work and representing HSC/E in Parliament. The Sponsorship Unit supports the Department in exercising these roles.

While the Unit has general sponsorship and policy responsibility for HSC/E, other government departments retain the lead in a number of policy areas. In these situations HSC/E operates as the lead department's agent in the field under an Agency Agreement and/or a Memorandum of Understanding.

**The Sponsorship Unit supports the Department in exercising these roles.**

# 05 CORPORATE AND SHARED SERVICES

## Human Resources

### Strategy

**291.** The Department's workforce is a key enabler of the achievement of its objectives. To support delivery of the Department's ambitious work agenda and realise the benefits of modernisation investment, the overall business strategy for 2005–06 included a move towards a smaller workforce which is: more highly skilled; better motivated and rewarded; delivering improved levels of customer service, and at a lower unit cost.

**292.** The Department's people strategy has therefore been to put in place the programmes and initiatives to deliver this goal, through developing capability, managing the workforce, developing new performance and attendance management systems and ensuring that all staff have an opportunity to contribute to our goals. In addition the Department has continued modernising the Human Resources (HR) function to meet business needs and implemented a new approach to delivering HR services.

**293.** The strategic goal in HR for 2005–06 was, and remains, to enable managers to achieve their business goals through their people, and to help their people to achieve their potential to deliver business results and lead fulfilling working lives.

### Priorities in 2005–06

**294.** Within this overall strategy, the key priorities were to:

- enable the Department to meet its performance and customer service goals by continually developing the expertise and capability of all staff and recruiting the right people;
- improve the well-being and motivation of staff, based on a policy framework which is fair, flexible, accessible and business-focused;
- help the Department meet its modernisation goals by delivering a workforce management process that enables it to match its staff numbers to its business needs;
- help the Department to meet its people and organisational goals by providing the high quality and efficient HR services needed for today and becoming a strategic enabler for tomorrow's changes; and
- integrate and improve the HR service to the Department through delivery of the HR Modernisation Programme.

## Developments in 2005–06

### Building Capability

**295.** The Department's Skills Strategy, strongly aligned with the Civil Service-wide Professional Skills for Government initiative[86], has six steps:

- an understanding of the capabilities the Department needs in order to achieve its goals, now and in the future;
- clarity about the capability requirements for job roles, expressed through skills/competences, and where appropriate, experience and accreditation;
- a common language and framework for all capability requirements, providing transparency for lateral and vertical progression;
- line managers and individual members of staff taking responsibility, through the Performance and Development System, for identifying individual development needs and reviewing progress towards achieving them;
- a flexible and responsive learning and development system, providing access through portals to a cost-effective mix of training opportunities and learning materials to meet individual needs; and
- continuing evaluation of the Department's capability requirements and the effectiveness of investment in learning and development.

**296.** Work to build the infrastructure necessary to support implementation of the Skills Strategy has included development of capability requirements, including role profile templates, plans for a Dictionary of Competencies, and a new competency framework for Grades 7 and above, based on Professional Skills for Government. Self assessment against this framework took place for all Grades 7 and above at mid-year review.

**297.** Modernisation of learning and development has continued with the establishment of a blended learning content fund, of which £9 million was allocated to specific projects on a return on investment basis. The Department spent an estimated £175 million on learning and development in 2005–06. As part of its strategy to evaluate the impact of this expenditure, each business has identified a single high-level Learning and Development priority and a senior sponsor will certify the business aims that it will support, the success criteria to be applied, and whether these criteria have been met. The Department is an accredited Investor in People and will be reassessed for accreditation at the end of 2006.

**298.** This year saw the first Department-wide review of senior talent, which was conducted to assess the capacity of the Department's senior leaders, and identify and develop those Senior Civil Servants (SCS) with high potential. An initiative to do the same for people in feeder grades to the SCS was also piloted. Developmental provision for leaders is through the Leadership Excellence Action Programme and this has proved very

**86** psg.civilservice.gov.uk/

successful, with over 70 per cent of the target audience using the programme.

**299.** A bespoke accelerated development programme was delivered to high potential SCS members.

**300.** The Leadership and Management Portal (LaMP) provides online access to learning. Over 50,000 visits were made to the site during the year and businesses are increasingly incorporating LaMP products into their development plans.

**301.** The training in IT applications, which was made available online last year, has proved popular, with over 14,000 people undertaking at least one course.

### Workforce Management

**302.** The Department is putting in place a modern, efficient organisation that will need fewer staff. Building on significant levels of modernisation investment, efficiency plans are based on a net reduction of 30,000 staff from March 2004 through to March 2008.

**303.** A central aim in taking forward the efficiency programme is the deployment of a workforce strategy, which seeks to ensure security of employment for as many appropriately skilled staff as possible who want to remain with the Department. The workforce strategy is underpinned by an agreement with Departmental trade unions, which seeks to avoid compulsory redundancy through a number of agreed measures.

**304.** Cross-business regional planning networks are actively managing the redeployment of surplus staff. The Department is also working closely with Cabinet Office and other departments to maximise re-deployment opportunities across the Civil Service. To date, around 50 per cent of surplus staff have been redeployed either to other jobs in the Department (42 per cent) or to other departments (8 per cent).

**305.** The Department is also running a number of voluntary early release/retirement schemes where this is proved to be cost effective. Volunteers for early release leave the Department on early severance or retirement under agreed Civil Service-wide conditions.

### Improving Selection Processes

**306.** The Department has continued to maintain tight controls on external recruitment, but has recruited externally where specific skills are not already available internally, or turnover is high due to a competitive market in specific locations.

**307.** The Department continues to improve its selection process. In October 2005 the system was reviewed to assess people's skills and abilities, and incorporate the new Departmental competencies, putting the emphasis on selecting people for the Department's future needs. It remains a flexible, inclusive system, encouraging applications from all groups in society. A full review of the system has started and is due to be completed early in 2006–07.

**The Department is an accredited Investor in People and will be reassessed for accreditation at the end of 2006.**

**308.** Work is underway to integrate the new Professional Skills for Government framework into external selection. This will affect all grades AA-G6 and the changes will be introduced during the coming year.

**309.** The Department's selection system is subject to rigorous internal audit and its recruitment practices are also assessed by the Civil Service Commissioners. This year saw the introduction of the new compliance monitoring process introduced by the Commissioners. This takes the form of self-assessment by the Department of the risk of its recruitment policy and practices not complying with the Recruitment Code. The Commissioners review the self assessment and provide their view on the Department's recruitment system. The Department has been assessed as low risk.

## The Department as a New Deal Employer

**310.** As the Department has responsibility for New Deal, it seeks to be the lead public sector employer of New Deal participants.

**311.** The Department's New Deal Employment Option is open to applicants from any New Deal programme. The programme's aim is to give the individual the skills, confidence and competencies to gain permanent employment, either within the Department or with another employer.

**312.** The controls on external recruitment at Administrative Assistant/Officer (the levels at which the Department takes people onto the New Deal programme) have had an impact on recruitment to the programme. In 2004–05 the number had fallen to 29 people employed on the programme, with a similar number in 2005–06. However, arrangements are in place to increase the Department's New Deal intake in line with any increases in external recruitment activity.

## Managing Attendance

**313.** The Department has made considerable progress in reducing its sickness absence levels. In the 12 months up to February 2005, the average number of days lost due to ill health was 12.5 days per employee year. For the 12 months up to February 2006 this reduced to 10.4 days, a 17 per cent reduction over the period. The in-month figure in February 2006 was 9.1, compared to 12.7 in February 2005, which illustrates the continuing improvement in this area.

**314.** The Department has achieved this success by taking a range of steps in line with the recommendations in the report from the Ministerial Task Force for Health, Safety and Productivity, *Managing Sickness Absence in the Public Sector*, published in November 2004.[87] These included:

- raising employee awareness of the senior management team's commitment to reducing sickness absences, by launching a revised attendance management policy in July 2005;

- enabling managers to intervene before absence levels cause concern, by giving them online access to individual employees' attendance records;

87 www.hse.gov.uk/gse/sickness.pdf

- rolling out a new IT system to provide managers (from office to Departmental level) with quicker and better data about absence levels, and the action being taken;
- ensuring line managers complied fully with the processes for managing cases of poor attendance; and
- taking action within the operational businesses to bring to a conclusion the worst cases of long term absence.

### Health and Safety

**315.** The Department aspires to the highest standards in health and safety performance. It does this through the application of a robust risk management framework to ensure resources are appropriately targeted at areas of significant risk. During 2005-06, work continued to modernise health and safety systems, increase line manager capability and improve compliance with the Department's health and safety policies. Measures introduced include:

- the appointment of dedicated health and safety co-ordinators in each of the businesses to improve policy compliance and the monitoring of performance;
- the setting up of a co-ordinators group to enable good practice to be shared across the Department;
- closer working between the business health and safety leads at board level, to ensure health and safety issues are taken into account in business strategies;
- the introduction of new health and safety training for all line managers;
- the piloting of self service online e-learning for Display Screen Equipment training; and
- the establishment of an extensive network of health and safety committees to enable full consultation and discussion of health and safety issues between the Department and the trade unions.

### Diversity and Equality

**316.** Diversity and Equality aims and objectives are central to the Department's mission of independence and equality for all. There are four key goals:

- To provide the best possible services to all the Department's customers, reflecting their diverse range of requirements.
- To build a workforce that reflects, and is part of, the wider community, and be an employer of choice in a diverse market place.
- To enable all staff to maximise their potential to contribute to business objectives.
- To enable the Department's external partners to provide services to the same high standard.

### Key achievements in 2005–06 include:

- publication of *Realising Equality in the Department for Work and Pensions* on 1 August[88], which was the first time the Department had reported on all aspects of diversity in one publication;

88 www.dwp.gov.uk/publications/dwp/2005/rre05/

- development of Disability Confident, an interactive learning package which provides information on the best way to interact with disabled customers and employees;
- a gold award in the Race for Opportunity benchmarking, coming third in the top 10 public sector performers;
- achieving third place in the Stonewall Equality Index of top 100 employers for lesbian, gay and bisexual staff; and
- the provision of high quality guidance to all the Department's employees, including a video Getting it Right which supports them in handling sexual orientation issues and civil partnerships.

**317.** Figure 30 below illustrates the Department's progress towards its targets for a diverse workforce.

Figure 30 **Progress against equality targets**

**Ethnicity Targets – percentage of minority groups by grade**

| Grade | March 2008 target | Position at 30 September 2003 | Position at 30 September 2004 | Position at 30 September 2005 |
|---|---|---|---|---|
| SCS | 5% | 2.2% | 3.3% | 3.7% |
| G6/G7 | 4% | 2.0% | 2.8% | 3.2% |
| SEO | 4% | 2.0% | 3.2% | 3.6% |
| HEO | 5.5% | 3.2% | 4.4% | 4.9% |

**Disability Targets – percentage of disabled people by grade**

| Grade | March 2008 target | Position at 30 September 2003 | Position at 30 September 2004 | Position at 30 September 2005 |
|---|---|---|---|---|
| SCS | 6% | 4.8% | 5.0% | 4.8% |
| G6/G7/SEO | 4% | 4.0% | 3.8% | 4.0% |
| HEO/EO | 7% | 6.4% | 6.1% | 6.5% |
| AO/AA | 6% | 4.7% | 4.5% | 4.6% |

**Gender Targets – percentage of women by grade**

| Grade | March 2008 target | Position at 30 September 2003 | Position at 30 September 2004 | Position at 30 September 2005 |
|---|---|---|---|---|
| SCS | 38% | 33.3% | 33.5% | 32.7% |
| G6 | 45% | 40.3% | 40.3% | 42% |
| G7 | 45% | 42.7% | 43.7% | 44.7% |

## Pay and Reward

**318.** The Department successfully implemented the second year of the three-year pay deal agreed with the unions in 2004. This has provided greater certainty for staff and, at the same time, enabled the Department to continue to make real progress towards its reward strategy:

- pay scales are continuing to be shortened and pay scale minima are becoming more competitive in the market;
- the system introduced in 2003-04 for assessing the performance of individuals has been improved and consolidated;
- individual performance bonuses have continued to be paid at the higher levels established in 2004, with clear links to the performance management system;
- for the first time some line managers have been given discretion in the award of bonuses; and
- there are four different pay zones to reflect different market conditions across the country.

**319.** The Department has started work on a review of the existing Reward Strategy.

## Employee Relations

**320.** In 2005–06 the Department reviewed its arrangements for consulting and keeping the trade unions up to date on developments. The unions were fully engaged in the review process and discussions on the outcomes continue. In addition, the Department has consulted its trade unions extensively on a wide range of major issues including its workforce planning programme, HR modernisation and efficiency challenges.

**321.** The early part of 2006 was marked by industrial action by one of the three trade unions, over the Department's modernisation programme and workforce planning strategy. The Department is ready to continue discussions with the unions on implementation of its modernisation programme and to engage them on day-to-day business, actively seeking to build a better working relationship with them.

## HR Modernisation

**322.** The HR Modernisation Programme harnesses industry best practice and investment in technology to improve the way HR services are delivered across the Department and to help make significant efficiencies. Activities in 2005-06 included:

- implementation of key elements of the HR Service Delivery Model, including HR Business Partners taking on a more strategic role;
- good progress on the rationalisation of the network of HR Service Centres (ultimately in 2006-07 to two sites) delivering a more effective and efficient service to line managers and staff, with key performance indicators for timeliness, quality and customer satisfaction in place;

**The Department successfully implemented the second year of the three-year pay deal agreed with the unions in 2004.**

- piloting a new HR Customer Support Service;
- full implementation of the staff information system, delivering self service functionality for sickness absence and booking learning; and
- simplified and improved HR policies making them more business- and customer-focused, accessible and viable.

## Finance

### Introduction

**323.** The Department is one of the largest financial organisations anywhere:

- it has financial transactions with 17 million customers every week;
- it pays out more than £115 billion a year in social security benefits;
- it recovers over £450 million a year through its Debt Management activities.
- in 2005-06, the Department's operating and programme budget of £8.7 billion incorporated a significant programme of information systems and technology change; and
- of that amount, it spent more than £4 billion a year on goods and services from external suppliers.

**324.** Finance is a key enabler in helping the Department to achieve its key departmental goals and social policy objectives and outcomes.

### Strategy

**325.** To ensure that Finance continues to meet the needs of its customers across the Department, an integrated programme of activity which is fundamentally transforming the way in which Finance delivers its business began to roll out throughout 2005–06. This activity continues into 2006–07.

**326.** The Finance Transformation Programme will;

- improve the ability of the Department to manage value for money;

- provide cost-effective, customer-focused business and administration processes and services to the Department;
- ensure everyone is clear about their accountabilities, what decisions they can make and how to manage risk, performance and compliance;
- maximise the benefits from existing technology programmes;
- increase the resource awareness and resource management capability of the Department's staff; and
- build a finance community that displays the behaviours its customers want to see.

### Priorities for 2005–2008

**327.** The Department's finance community has a series of challenging targets for 2005–2008. These are to:

- deliver an effective planning and performance management framework across the Department;
- implement a commercial strategy that allows the Department to improve and sustain value for money and improve services with regard to procurement and supply of third party goods and services;
- deliver a fully integrated finance, procurement and HR shared services capability, benchmarked with other government and commercial shared services and delivering a programme of improvement to provide value for money services to the Department and certain other government departments;
- make accurate payments to customers and promote effective value for money controls;
- ensure that managers across the Department have the capability and skills to take appropriate financial decisions and manage the Department's financial records;
- ensure that cross-departmental financial risks are understood and managed; and
- implement a fully risk-based approach to our assurance deliverables to assure the Accounting Officers of the Department's ability to meet objectives.

### Developments in 2005–06

### Planning and performance management

**328.** As part of the Department's Finance Transformation Programme the Integrated Planning and Performance Management strand has introduced new frameworks for Departmental planning and performance management. These are designed to ensure the integration of financial and non-financial planning and performance management, with a consistent approach across the whole Department including its agencies. Developments during 2005–06 include the design of a new integrated planning model, and the implementation of a Departmental balanced scorecard for the Executive Team which reports progress towards the Department's top-level strategic and cross-cutting objectives.

### Resource Management

**329.** The Department is implementing an integrated finance, procurement, human resources and payroll system based on Oracle e-business software.

**330.** The introduction of this 'Resource Management' system is a major undertaking and reflects the significant investment being made to improve operational efficiency, control and level of decision making, both individual and corporate.

**331.** The four-stage implementation programme commenced in December 2005. To date the first two stages have been completed allowing staff across the Department to use this new system to carry out financial and procurement processes.

## Commercial Strategy

**332.** The Department is responding positively to the procurement challenges set in the Efficiency Review. The strategic approach, collaboration with other Government departments and a challenging procurement modernisation programme have allowed good progress to be made against all ten targets for the Department's commercial function set out in the Commercial Strategy.

**333.** For example, the Department has made the biggest contribution to the Office of Government Commerce (OGC) targets to deliver value-for-money savings through improved procurement. In 2004–05 the Department reported procurement value-for-money gains of £326.4 million to OGC, this was 7.6 per cent of all expenditure with external suppliers and 29.5 per cent of the total gains reported by all Departments. This allowed OGC to exceed its target of £3 billion in value for money savings a year early.

**334.** The Commercial Strategy target to achieve 75 per cent professionally-qualified staff in key procurement posts by 2007 was met a year early, with the proportion increased from 67 per cent in 2004 to reach 75 per cent in December 2005.

**335.** In line with the Government's timetable, the Department launched its Sustainable Development strategy in December 2005. This sets out how the Department will use its purchasing power and market influence to further the Government's economic, social and environmental policy objectives.

## Shared Services

**336.** The Shared Services Project has completed all the options analysis and design work necessary for the creation of the new Shared Services organisation early in 2006–07.

**337.** Final decisions are imminent around the governance, client relationship management and financial regime to enable the new organisation to operate in a true shared service manner.

## Accurate payments and effective value for money controls

## Central Payment System

**338.** The Department has established a project to implement an integrated payment and accounting capability for its business and improve its business continuity capability for serious system failure.

**339.** The Central Payment System Project has made excellent progress during 2005–06. The procurement exercise to obtain a highly resilient and efficient integrated payments and accounting system has been successfully concluded and the project is moving towards implementation stage, with plans to go live in April 2008 and complete full rollout in 2010.

### Payment Modernisation Programme (PMP)

**340.** The Department has modernised the way it pays pensions and benefits. Order books have been phased out, and it now pays 97 per cent of customers directly into an account.

**341.** An enabling project for PMP, the Local Payment System has modernised (and automated) the production and accounting for cheques as well as creating the ability to trigger direct payments at payment offices.

### Debt Management

**342.** The Department consolidated its newly centralised Debt Management organisation with the rollout, in August 2005, of the commercially developed IT system, Debt Manager.

**343.** The Department's successful relationship with the private sector in seeking recovery of debt is continuing, with the pilot achieving recoveries of £22.6 million since April 2004.

### Improving Financial Control

**344.** The Department needs to demonstrate the highest standards of financial management and control. The Department's accounts continue to be qualified mainly because of significant levels of fraud and error in benefit awards and significant uncertainties over certain debtor and creditor balances. The accounts have also been qualified this year due to an Excess Vote.

**345.** The action being taken to tackle fraud and error set out in Chapter Three should help address this situation. Financial control requirements for all new IT systems are being specified and agreed well before approval to proceed on system development is authorised. The Department has taken action to enhance internal control to prevent Excess Vote problems in future years.

### Departmental Investment Strategy[89]

**346.** The Departmental Investment Strategy is primarily focused on bringing about significant improvements in both customer service and operational efficiencies, with investment incurred principally in two areas:

- a programme to provide modern, fit-for-purpose information technology and information systems; and
- strategic investment in the Department's estate to provide a far more welcoming environment for those clients who receive their customer service in person.

**347.** In the area of information systems and telephony there continues to be rapid advancement in technology and software. The strategy recognises the need to stay up-to-date and make provision in future years to refresh the infrastructure.

**348.** Strategic investment is managed through a number of projects with progress being monitored on a monthly basis.

## The Department is responding positively to the procurement challenges set in the Efficiency Review.

89 www.dwp.gov.uk/publications/dwp/2005/invest_strategy.pdf

Figure 31 **Investment plans from 2005 to 2008**

| Year | 2005–06 | 2006–07 | 2007–08 | SR 2004 |
|---|---|---|---|---|
| Level of investment (£ million) | 1,126 | 1,283* | 529* | **2,938** |

Note: These are revised Departmental Capital forecasts and Change Programme 'one off' resource forecasts as at 31 December 2005, updating the SR 2004 figures published in the Departmental Investment Strategy, with End Year Flexibilities from 2004–05.

* CSA Operational Improvement Plan forecasts have not been included, as these are awaiting approval by the Department's Investment Committee following Ministerial announcements.

## Building Capability

**349.** An extensive Department-wide learning and development programme to increase resource awareness and resource management skill and capability within the Department is rolling out. This includes new learning and development products to ensure that the Department can fully exploit the capabilities afforded through the Resource Management System.

## Managing Risk

**350.** The Department continues to improve its capability to manage risks. The latest formal risk assessment exercise, conducted in June 2005, concluded that risk was defined, and that strategies and policies were in place and communicated across the Department. Plans are in place to drive further improvement, as the management of risk is integrated into routine business processes and consistency of approach is achieved across all areas of the business.

## Assurance

**351.** The Department has modernised its assurance planning process and has agreed a new risk-based planning approach with the Departmental Audit Committee for 2006–07.

## Estate Strategy

**352.** In addition to the priorities outlined earlier the Department has continued to make progress with its Estate Strategy, which covers the Department's approach to modernising the estate, meeting targets to reduce the size and cost of the estate and improving space utilisation. Good progress has been made to reduce the size of the estate in line with the Department's workforce efficiency challenge. The size of the Department's estate at February 2006 was 2.447 million square metres, a reduction of over 200,000 square metres since April 2004. It is projected that the estate will reduce to 2.38 million square metres by March 2006.

**353.** A number of major estates projects were completed during the year, all of which met or exceeded the Achieving Excellence in Construction targets[90]; including a significant contribution in helping the Department meet the requirements of the Disability Discrimination Act. Public access work programmes, fully funded by Land Securities Trillium through the estates PFI contract and costing around £4 million, have been completed at some 1,032 sites across the estate.

**90** www.ogc.gov.uk/index.asp?id=218

**354.** A £2.2 billion programme to deliver a fully integrated work and benefit service through a network of new and completely refurbished Jobcentre Plus offices will be largely complete by the end of March, with the remainder in 2006–07.

**355.** The programme of office refurbishments, acquisitions and disposals accounts for £1 billion of the £2.2 billion and is one of the biggest change programmes attempted in the public sector or elsewhere. In recognition, of this the Department won the prestigious Integrated Supply Chain Team of the Year Award, sponsored by Building Magazine in 2005, and was short-listed also for the Construction Best Practice Award.

**356.** Work has started to deliver a network of around 77 Benefit Delivery Centres that will centralise benefit processing functions, previously delivered in around 650 offices, by 2008, and this will complete the Jobcentre Plus modernisation programme.

## Information Technology and Programme Management

**357.** Information Technology (IT) is critical to the successful delivery of the Government's welfare reform agenda. It enables the Department to develop its services to customers – processing claims, make payments, helping people into jobs – while achieving its efficiency challenge. IT is also at the heart of the Department's change programme, one of the largest in Europe. The Department is modernising its services, supported by a major investment programme in IT-enabled services for its customers and staff. It is also transforming its IT capability and the relationship with its suppliers, to produce better services and value.

**358.** Efficient and reliable service delivery relies on high performing IT. The essential task is to maintain and improve one of the largest IT systems in the world to enable businesses to deliver to customers. The Department continues to work with suppliers to ensure IT problems are minimised. When problems do occur, business continuity arrangements are in place to minimise disruption.

### Strategy

**359.** The Department's strategic approach to Information Systems and Information Technology (IS/IT) was developed in 2002. The Department is applying its principles of smaller projects based on commercial-off-the-shelf packages and the integration of new IT applications with existing legacy systems. The strategy is under review as part of a cyclical programme of strategy development. A report is due in the summer of 2006 which will set out the Department's vision for information systems until 2015 and how that vision will be delivered.

### Sourcing Strategy

**360.** Effective management of the procurement of the Department's IT equipment and its service providers is central to the Department's IS/IT transformation agenda. The Department made major progress on its IT sourcing strategy during 2005-06. A key achievement is the realignment of existing contracts with Electronic Data Systems (EDS) and British Telecom (BT) to fit this framework. This will deliver services based on industry-wide standards and supplied at competitive market prices, and drive up supplier performance. The Sourcing Strategy will achieve this by:

- simplifying the contractual and commercial arrangements and the supporting sourcing processes;
- delivering greater value for money and supporting the efficiency agenda; and
- creating a more competitive external market while facilitating collaboration between these suppliers to support current and emerging business needs.

**361.** In line with this strategy, the Department has continued to adhere to the IT contractual frameworks established under the UNderpinning IT DeliverY (Unity) Project. These enable the Department to access a range of suppliers with diverse skills and quickly set up contracts to deliver specific business requirements.

### Channel Strategy

**362.** The Department is working to ensure that services are developed and delivered in ways which better reflect its customers' contact channel preferences, needs and experiences, and are marketed efficiently.

**363.** The Department has already moved to deliver its services via sophisticated telephony systems (Pension Credit application line), online self-service systems (Jobsearch) many of which are delivered through Directgov or electronic data transfer (payment of benefits directly to customer's bank accounts). Most payments are now made through modern IT-enabled contact centres.

### The Modernisation Programme

**364.** Figure 32 lists the Department's current major IT-enabled programmes and projects with information on schedules, budgets, and purpose.

Figure 32 **The Department's modernisation programme**

| Project | Purpose and achievements to date | Start date | Planned end date | Current expected completion date | Current forecast cost £ million | Expenditure to date £ million |
|---|---|---|---|---|---|---|
| Benefit Processing Replacement Programme (Watch 2) | The programme provides a core IT platform with a lasting foundation for a modern IT system. It will increase the efficiency of systems for processing benefit, tackling fraud and working with employers. Customers will be able to access a range of services online. | Dec 2003 | Oct 2006 | Under review (see note 5) | Under review (see note 5) | 141 |
| Pensions Transformation Project | The programme will transform the way that The Pension Service delivers its business. The first wave of change involving new State Pension claim processes was deployed in three transformation sites by the end of 2005. | Jan 2002 | 2006 | 2010–11 | 707 | 308 |
| Customer Information System | This project will deliver a database of key citizen information to be shared across the Department. The database will complement information currently available in the Department's key customer information systems (the Personal Details Computer System and Departmental Central Index) and become their replacement. | July 2003 | July 2007 | July 2007 | 77 | 50 |

| Project | Purpose and achievements to date | Start date | Planned end date | Current expected completion date | Current forecast cost £ million | Expenditure to date £ million |
|---|---|---|---|---|---|---|
| Resource Management | This will provide modernised HR, financial and procurement functions for the Department. The automation of data and processes will save time and resources. Rollout of the new processes to users began in December 2005. | April 2001 | Nov 2006 | Nov 2006 | 185 | 163 |
| Debt Management | This programme aims to increase efficiency in recovering debt. All ten Debt Centres are set up and operational. All work was successfully migrated from 126 feeder sites into the Debt Centres by February 2006. | Nov 2000 | April 2005 | Feb 2006 | 103 | 102 |
| Central Payments System (formerly part of Payment Modernisation) | The Central Payments system is required to support the Department in processing payments for new entitlement management and financial scheduling systems. | April 2004 | March 2010 | March 2010 | 141 | 14 |

**Notes to Figure 32:**

1. This is a rolling programme of a number of business and IT improvement projects with individual start and completion dates.

2. The table includes only those projects which are predominantly IT-enabled and therefore excludes other, primarily business change, projects managed by the Change Delivery Committee. These are: Jobcentre Plus Centralisation of Benefit Processing; Jobcentre Plus Implementation; Building on New Deal; Disability and Carers Service Modernisation; Pensions Protection Fund; Department for Work and Pensions IT Transformation; Finance Transformation Programme; Human Resources Modernisation Programme.

3. The current forecast cost column provides forecasts of the investment required to project implementation. Expenditure on projects is formally approved by the Department's governance process and authorised through a series of formal reviews, to establish that projects are still meeting the expected standards.

4. Due end date is the completion date forecast in the first stages of a project or programme. Current expected completion date may change depending on factors such as: changes in scope, cost or quality. Such changes must be approved by the appropriate governance body. Any significant change to the expected completion date for projects in this table must be approved by the Department's Change Delivery Committee, chaired by the Chief Information Officer.

5. As part of the Benefit Processing Replacement Programme's governance, it was reviewed in February 2006. A number of options for taking forward the Programme were presented. A decision was made to review the situation again after four months, having considered the impact of the Welfare Reform Green Paper. Meanwhile, the investment programme would continue by taking forward work in areas common to all options presented. Agreed forecast costs and completion date are dependent upon this decision.

## Developments in 2005–06

### Key developments in modernisation

**365.** Significant progress has been made on delivering the benefits of the modernisation programme:

- The Department has continued to roll out the integrated Jobcentre Plus model with over 700 modern, customer-friendly offices now delivering a combination of benefit advice, welfare to work and job search. Rollout is expected to be substantially complete by summer 2006 – around 880 locations in total.

- The Payment Modernisation Programme has continued and 22.5 million accounts are now being paid directly into a bank or building society account, with over 97 per cent of customers paid by direct payment. The PSA target to make 85 per cent of payments by direct payment by December 2005 was met early. This payment method will save the taxpayer in excess of £1 billion over the next five years.

- The Pension Forecasting IT System, successfully launched in June 2005, offers customers the online provision of state pension forecasts and has reduced the number of staff currently required to carry out Future Pensions Centre functions. Pensions forecasting allows people to make an informed decision about their retirement.

- The first phase of the Customer Information System was launched in March 2005 and provides a single, accurate view of key information about the Department's customers, so that staff can provide them with a quick efficient service. Its objective is that customers will only have to give key information once. It has been implemented in phases throughout 2005–06 and now provides tailored online access service for local authorities, the Department for Constitutional Affairs, HM Court Services, the Northern Ireland Social Security Agency and the Driver and Vehicle Licensing Agency.

- Employer Direct online has been operating on a live national basis from May 2005. This system allows registered employers to post and manage vacancies themselves online. The vacancies appear in the job bank, where they can be accessed by jobseekers via the internet, Jobseeker Direct and Jobpoints. Over 14 per cent of all Jobcentre Plus vacancies are taken in this way.

### Transforming our suppliers

**366.** During 2005–06 the Department introduced a revised services framework. This sets out the map under which suppliers will deliver services to the Department in a manner which best fits their expertise and which will enable us to compare these services with equivalent market offerings. The Department has re-aligned its existing contracts with EDS, and those with BT, to fit this framework.

**367.** The agreement with EDS will mean that on average, over the next five years, the Department will be spending £520 million a year on services delivered by EDS. This compares to around £700 million a year spent in the Department's first full year (2002). The realigned BT contract means that, for no additional cost, the Department will be able to take advantage of the flexibility and effectiveness of BT's 21st Century Network programme, designed to transform the entire communications infrastructure in the UK by the end of this decade.

### Increasing internal capability

**368.** During 2005–06 the Department has put in place a plan to develop and implement new ways of working, reflecting industry best practice, and creating an efficient, professional team of IS/IT specialists.

**369.** During 2005–06 the Department has achieved:

- a smaller but highly skilled and experienced IT professional workforce, with numbers reduced from 1,273 in April 2004 to 515 in October 2005;
- key professional appointments made in a number of areas to increase capability, bringing a wealth of external expertise; and
- better engagement between the Department's businesses and its IS/IT professionals through Information System Directors, who report to the Chief Information Officer and business heads.

## Information, research and analysis

**370.** The Department has long recognised the need to build, monitor and evaluate policy and delivery around a sound evidence base, and its analytical work is recognised as being of the highest professional quality. The Department's evidence, research and analysis strategy[91] was approved by the Government Chief Scientist in 2005. Most of the work to support policy development and analysis is done within mixed teams of policy specialists and analysts. This is supported by two corporate Directorates:-

- The **Information Directorate** provides most of the Department's key data sources and outputs including national statistics, analytical databases, management information and data matching, primarily for fraud and error
- **Cross Cutting Strategy and Analysis Directorate** develops the Department's strategic direction, and undertakes supporting cross-cutting research and analysis, provides forecasts of expenditure and business workloads, and develops policy analysis models.

**The Department has made major improvements over recent years to its sources of information and to its capability to exploit them.**

91 www.dwp.gov.uk/asd5/ER&AStrategy.pdf

**371.** The Department has made major improvements over recent years to its sources of information and to its capability to exploit them. The main development has been a longitudinal client-based data set. This combines data from Department for Work and Pensions and HM Revenue and Customs sources and gives a picture of how individual clients move into and out of the benefits system and into employment. It is now one of the prime sources of research and analysis and is used for external reporting via national statistics.

**372.** The Department is also using this and other data sources to support directly the delivery of several of its key objectives, including:–

**373. Fraud and Accuracy:** Data matching and risk profiling work has helped the Department's fraud investigators to drive down fraud and error, with 36,000 cases referred to field units every month since April 2005. By March 2006 this will have revealed overpayments in excess of £80 million across the range of benefits. An additional 20,000 cases have been referred to local authorities every month. By the year-end this will have revealed overpayments in excess of £80 million within Housing Benefit and Council Tax Benefit.

**374. Benefit take-up:** Research into reasons for non-take-up of benefit and linking information across benefit systems has led to improvements in Pension Credit take-up. This has helped The Pension Service to move from 'blanket' mailing to targeted campaigns.

**375. Employment Targets:** Information Directorate data has been used for the successful pilots of the Job Outcome Target to measure Jobcentre Plus performance in helping customers into work. The Job Outcome Target will be introduced nationally from April 2006. Linking benefits data with HM Revenue and Customs P45/46 data informs the Department about customers moving into work. This provides a more relevant performance measure and:

- reduces staff resource on non-value added activities of capturing and validating performance;
- enables staff to refer customers to modernisation channels without losing performance; and
- encourages more efficient Adviser performance.

**376. Departmental strategy:** Cross-Cutting Strategy and Analysis Directorate is working with departmental businesses, policy teams and other government departments to develop and improve the Department's overarching outcome and business strategy. This is underpinned by a significant analytical work programme, to consider long-term challenges such as the ageing society and the effects of further globalisation, medium-term issues including the Department's business direction and its relationship with employers, as well as considering the short-term risks to business delivery.

**377. Policy analysis and financial planning:** Forecasts and projections of benefit expenditure and caseloads provide an essential foundation for the analysis of major policy reform, including pensions, incapacity benefits and housing benefits, as well as being a key element of the Government's overall financial planning. In recent years the Department has considerably developed and improved its forecasting and projection capability, culminating in the transfer of analytical functions from the Government Actuary's Department in respect of National Insurance Fund benefit forecasts. The Directorate also develops and maintains a number of models for policy analysis, and in the past year has delivered a ground-breaking new dynamic micro-simulation model, Pensim2, for the long-term analysis of pension policy, used significantly in the Pensions Commission final report published in autumn 2005.

**378. Business planning:** The Cross-Cutting Strategy and Analysis Directorate also provides business planning tools to the Department's businesses, including workload forecasts, longer-term forecasts to assist with development of the businesses' strategy, development of tools to accurately measure business productivity, and analysis to underpin the planning and management of the Department's workforce.

# 06 OTHER AREAS OF PUBLIC INTEREST

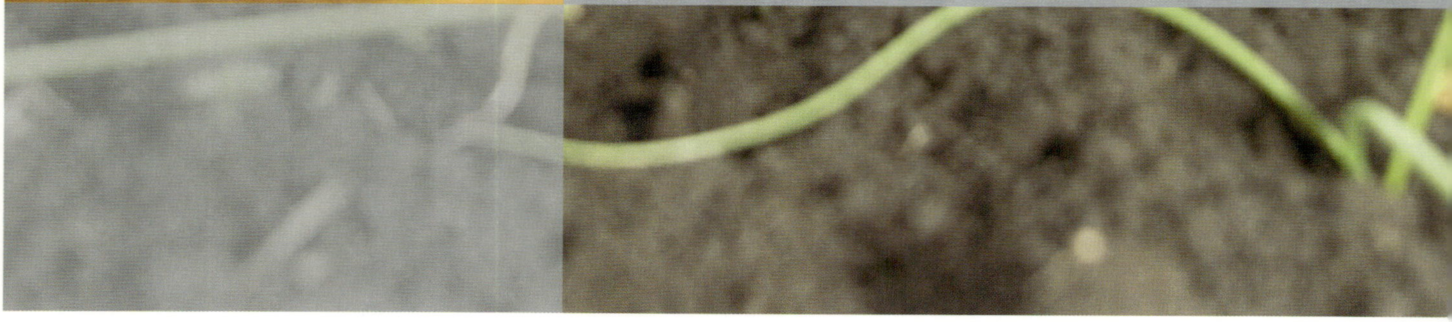

## Better regulation

379. The Department is committed to reducing existing regulatory burdens wherever possible, and to minimising the impact on business of any new legislation, including EU legislation.

380. It is important for the Department to strike the right balance between avoiding unnecessary burdens on business, charities and voluntary organisations, and protecting the interests of citizens.

381. Stephen Timms was the Department's Better Regulation Minister, with responsibility for promoting the better regulation agenda and for ensuring that regulations:

- are necessary;
- give effective protection;
- balance cost and risk;
- are fair; and
- command public confidence.

382. At board level, the Department's Director General of Strategy and Pensions oversees the Department's better regulation work. He is responsible for promoting better regulation in the Department, and for supporting the work of the Department's Better Regulation Unit (BRU) which is now part of the Department's Cross-cutting Strategy and Analysis Directorate. This places the BRU at the centre of the Department's strategic capability, helping to secure further improvements to the Department's better regulation performance by having direct access to analytical support.

383. The Department is committed to improving the quality of regulation. The Department's BRU continues to work with the Cabinet Office Better Regulation Executive, to raise departmental awareness of better regulation, and to improve the quality and use of Regulatory Impact Assessments (RIA).

384. Online information on a number of better regulation matters, including guidance on how to produce a RIA is available on the Department's intranet.

385. The Government's Better Regulation Action Plan[92] has dominated the Department's Better Regulation landscape this year, in particular the contribution to the Administrative Burdens Reduction (ABR) project led by the Cabinet Office Better Regulation Executive.

386. The Department has been very closely involved in measuring the administrative burden (for example, the cost of providing information and completing forms) placed upon business, charities and the voluntary sector.

387. A Department for Work and Pensions Better Regulation Stakeholder Group (the first in Whitehall), chaired by the Department's Better Regulation Minister, has been established to advise the Department and to help identify needlessly burdensome regulation and/or that which causes the most irritation.

92 www.cabinetoffice.gov.uk/regulation/documents/pdf/action_plan.pdf

388. The group has engaged directly with the Department on the ABR project. It has guided and monitored the Department's progress with it, identified stakeholders willing to participate in the project, and has undertaken scrutiny, challenge and validation functions.

389. The Department is developing a plan for simplifying regulatory burdens, and for removing those which are outdated and outmoded. Stakeholders have been invited to make proposals. A dedicated e-mail address[93] has been set up for stakeholders to submit well-reasoned proposals of simplification.

390. The Department has already completed an exercise to consolidate over 200 sets of Housing Benefit and Council Tax Benefit amending regulations into just four new sets, and revoking over 25 pages, of regulation. This attracted favourable comment from the House of Lords Select Committee on the Merits of Statutory Instruments which applauded the Department's efforts to clarify for users, this frequently amended area of law.

391. A dedicated benefit simplification team has been set up within the Department as a counter-weight to increasing complexity across the benefit system. The team will publish a guide to best practice for ensuring that consideration is given to simplicity in the development of benefit changes and will work at reducing compexity in existing systems. This work will be informed by an understanding of how the system works for customers, their advocates, other service users, and staff who administer benefits.

392. Employer Direct online has been introduced to provide business with round-the-clock access to job vacancies on one of the largest, and most visited, job websites in the UK. This makes it easy to create, amend, close or re-advertise job vacancies quickly. This service has won a prestigious national e-government award.

393. Generally, the Department for Work and Pensions is not a major regulatory department. During 2005–06, the Department introduced no bills to Parliament but it brought forward 142 sets of regulations, very few of which resulted in new costs to business. Regulation which does have a significant impact on business, charities or the voluntary sector is supported by a Regulatory Impact Assessment (RIA).

394. The Department continues to achieve 100 per cent compliance with the RIA process, which underpins policy development work and assists ministers' consideration of policy options.

395. The RIA process has assisted in clarifying the Department's negotiations in Europe. The Department's initial RIA on the impact of the draft EU Directive on the portability of occupational pensions enabled the Department, under the UK's Presidency of the EU, to instigate a discussion at European level of the Commission's impact assessment. The initial RIA also identified key issues for the UK and has shaped the negotiations. It has also assisted in identifying those issues for stakeholders by accompanying the Department's consultation document on the proposed Directive, and provided an opportunity for stakeholders to refine the analysis and provide additional supporting material.

93 simplification@dwp.gsi.gov.uk

396. Where it has been necessary to regulate, the Department has consulted those affected by the legislation at an early stage, considering the views expressed, responding positively to suggestions and altering proposals accordingly where appropriate. The Department issues formal consultation documents and, in many cases, draft legislation.

397. The Department has also continued to consult local authorities in accordance with the central local partnership agreement between government and local authorities.

398. The Department has undertaken a number of full public consultations, each of which lasted at least 12 weeks in accordance with the Cabinet Office's code of practice on consultation.

399. In a number of instances, when dealing with specialised issues, ministers exercised their discretion not to conduct formal consultation exercises under the code of practice. However, these more limited consultations adopted best practice from the code.

400. For example, limited consultations aimed primarily at the pensions industry have been informed by ongoing discussions with industry representatives on pensions issues who, on a number of occasions, were contacted to agree a suitable period over which to invite responses. By engaging with the appropriate experts in a continuing dialogue, improvements have been made to the drafting of regulations including identification of potential unintended consequences.

401. Consultees are invited to comment to the Department's consultation co-ordinator on the process of consultation. The Department routinely identifies in its consultation documents when the Government's response is likely to be published. As with final RIAs, all consultation documents are published on the Department's website.

402. The Department has continued to make effective use of its stakeholder management arrangements and public consultation expertise to promote better policy making and improved service delivery. Pensions, welfare, and disability issues have featured in major public consultation exercises.

403. A mixture of focus groups, four regional events, and a leaflet and e-consultation have been used to obtain the views of disabled people and their representatives on two key proposals – the formation of an Office for Disability Issues and a National Forum for Organisations of Disabled People. Responding to the diverse range of information received, an advisory group of disabled people has been formed to advise ministers on the formation of a National Forum for Disabled People.

404. The welfare reform Green Paper – *A new deal for disabled people: Empowering people to work* has seen the production of a wide-ranging document which has generated considerable interest among customers and their representatives. Working with the Hansard Society, an online discussion forum to broaden public engagement has been developed.

405. The National Pensions Day on 18 March 2006 broke new ground for the Department with its consultations on proposals for future pensions reform. This large-scale exercise was run on deliberative engagement principles which provided participants with facts and information and time to discuss and think critically about the issues before them, in order to come to informed views. This new form of consultation is widely recognised as promoting wider public engagement in the democratic process.

406. Over one thousand people participated on the day in six satellite-linked events in England, Scotland, Wales and Northern Ireland. The discussions of a representative cross-section of the public were heard directly by the whole Department for Work and Pensions ministerial team along with ministers from other departments and the three Pensions Commissioners.

407. Wider debate was promoted through a dedicated website which included background material, video links and an online survey based on materials used in the deliberative events. A 'stakeholder toolkit' was also provided which allowed organisations to run events to explore the Pensions Commission's proposals.

408. The Department's agencies and independent regulators also follow the principles of better regulation. For example, The Pensions Regulator moved work-based pension regulation towards a flexible and proportionate regulatory approach, targeting its resources on those areas where scheme members' benefits are at greatest risk. In fulfilling its objectives of protecting members' benefits, the Regulator has made use of enhanced information gathering powers to implement this risk-based approach.

409. The size of the form used to gather pensions scheme information has been reduced by 50 per cent. Subsequent returns can be completed online and are pre-populated so that it is necessary to enter only changes since the last return was submitted.

410. The Regulator and the Pension Protection Fund are both represented on the Department's Better Regulation Stakeholder Group and have contributed to the Department's work on the Administrative Burdens Reduction project and development of the simplification plan.

411. The Department continues to consider alternatives to regulation. An example of this is The Pensions Regulator's issue of codes of practice providing practical guidelines on the requirements of pension legislation and setting out the standards of conduct and practice expected of those who must meet these requirements. The standards set out in the codes are consistent with how a well-run pension scheme would choose to meet its legal requirements.

412. The Health and Safety Commission/Executive, which is sponsored by the Department, publishes information about its better regulation performance in its annual report and accounts.[94]

94 www.hse.gov.uk/aboutus/reports/0405/index.htm

## Sustainable development

413. The Department continues to demonstrate its active support to the objectives of the *UK Strategy for Sustainable Development – Securing the Future*.[95] In September 2005, the Department produced a revised *Sustainable Development Policy Statement*, demonstrating commitment to the key priorities and principles of the new strategy. The Department's 23-point plan to deliver on its commitments, entitled *Delivering Sustainable Development – DWP Action Plan* was produced in December 2005.

414. The Action Plan will be carried forward by those appointed to the Sustainable Development Steering Group, part of the Executive Team sub-committee structure. The Steering Group is supported by a Network Group, which is representative of the whole Department, and is responsible for the actual delivery and implementation of positive actions.

415. One of the corner stones of incorporating sustainable development into routine business is that it is habitually addressed during all decision making processes. Building on the work already done in this area, guidance has been revised and made accessible on the Department's intranet. The Sustainable Development Minister hosted a conference for senior managers in January 2006 to further develop knowledge and understanding of what is required of decision makers.

416. A significant decision making area is that of procurement. The Department's *Sustainable Procurement Strategy* was produced in December 2005. Messages were consolidated at a conference in December, attended by key staff involved in securing goods and services for the Department, and a national programme of awareness events is under way.

417. To monitor progress, audits have been commissioned to specifically address how businesses are incorporating and recording sustainable development in their decisions, and the findings will enable further training to be targeted on weak areas.

418. Staff engagement is also key to delivering the objectives and to embedding sustainable development in to all Departmental functions. A variety of methods have been employed to capture staff interest on a broad basis. The intranet remains the main route through which communications can be made available to staff directly. A host of information is available, from formal publications such as the *Action Plan* and the *DWP Sustainable Development Annual Report*[96] to the e-magazine, Greenlines. This is designed to be eye-catching and light-hearted in approach to attract a wider audience.

**The focus is now moving to the reduction of overall energy consumption.**

95 www.sustainable-development.gov.uk/publications/uk-strategy/uk-strategy-2005.htm

96 www.dwp.gov.uk/sus-dev/2005/sus-dev05.pdf

419. Although the Department is moving away from paper-based communications, the new Policy Statement has been produced in both electronic and printed format. This is to encourage its display in all Departmental buildings, with its bright format and easy-to-understand text maximising staff awareness.

420. Communication with other government departments is maintained by active involvement in cross-government bodies such as the Sustainable Operations Board and the Sustainable Development Forum, to enable the development of government-wide targets and sharing of best practice.

421. There are four main operational areas that have been subject to much activity and will remain the Department's priority areas in the coming year. These are the reduction of carbon emissions, closely linked with reducing energy consumption, waste reduction and recycling and reduction in water consumption.

422. Efforts to reduce carbon emissions from travel have been targeted through the improvements in fleet cars, with an increasing number of alternatively fuelled cars and a reduction in mileage. Measures have also been put in place to capture relevant data regarding departmental air travel, enabling the Department to take part in the Government's Carbon Offsetting Scheme.

423. A number of improvements have been achieved by working with the Department's estate partners, Land Securities Trillium, including securing 60 percent of electricity supplies from renewable sources. The electricity has been generated from various sources, including wind, landfill gas and combined heat and power. The focus is now moving to the reduction of overall energy consumption, which has continued to rise as a result of modernising access to services by the introduction of more IT.

424. An initiative which will positively affect three of the Department's priorities will be the expansion of an automated utility meter-reading system. This will provide half-hourly readings for larger buildings, which use up to 85 per cent of the utilities supplied to the Department. This will enable better management of supplies, enable usage to be targeted and anomalies addressed quickly.

425. Waste production has continued to rise over the past year, but 52 per cent of that waste was recycled. Campaigns to minimise initial waste production and increase the amount of waste recycled will be launched in 2006–07.

426. The Department's achievements were recognised externally by Building Magazine's *Sustainable Client of the Year* award and the award of a Green Apple (Gold) for Environmental Best Practice. Further achievements and progress are reported annually in the *DWP Sustainable Development Annual Report*.

## International relations

427. The Joint International Unit, which serves both the Department for Work and Pensions and the Department for Education and Skills, has continued throughout 2005–06 to promote internationally the Government's policies for:

- increasing employment and reducing unemployment;
- combating social exclusion;
- ensuring the sustainability of pensions systems; and
- developing a skilled and adaptable workforce.

### European Union

428. In the course of the United Kingdom Presidency of the European Union in the second half of 2005, the Department played a key role in the economic reform, employment and social policy agenda. Specifically, the Department played a key role in the preparations for the Informal Summit of Heads of State and Government, by hosting the Tripartite Social Summit in October 2005, and made a significant contribution to the UK EU Presidency Conference on Corporate Social Responsibility.

429. In the coming year, the Department will build on the successful Presidency by contributing to the reform agenda agreed at the Hampton Court informal Summit. In particular it will work closely with the Austrian and Finnish Presidencies to keep up the pace of work. The main focus for the Department will be work concerning demographic changes over the next 25 years and their effect on employment, unemployment and pensions.

### European Social Fund

430. The Joint International Unit continued to manage the 2000–2006 European Social Fund (ESF) programme in England and the Equal programme in Great Britain to support policies to extend employment opportunities to all. Significant achievements were:

- ESF invested £602 million in projects, which helped over 560,000 people in England to improve their employability and skills. Funds were targeted at improving the prospects of people at a disadvantage in the labour market. About 55 per cent of participants were in work or entered further training when they completed their ESF-funded provision.
- In the second and final round of Equal, 98 new ESF-funded Development Partnerships continued work to develop new ways to combat discrimination and inequalities faced by disadvantaged groups in the labour market.

### International

431. In dealings with the wider world, the Joint International Unit:

- successfully co-ordinated the UK's participation in key events such as the G8 Labour and Employment Ministers Meeting, the International Labour Organisation (ILO) regional and international Conferences, and the second US/UK Dialogue on Pensions; and
- co-ordinated production of timely reports on UK compliance with the requirements of ILO instruments (Conventions and Recommendations) and the Council of Europe Social Charter.

Figure 33 **Volume of letters received and performance in replying to letters from MPs/Peers to Ministers and those sent directly to agency chief executives and senior business directors**

| | Target (working days) | Number of letters received | Performance[97] |
|---|---|---|---|
| Letters from MPs/Peers to Ministers | 20 | 10,596* | 90%** |
| Child Support Agency | 15 | 5,367 | 99% |
| Jobcentre Plus | 15 | 1,062 | 90% |
| The Pension Service | 15 | 1,042 | 98% |
| Disability and Carers Service | 15 | 425 | 100% |
| Health and Safety Executive | 15 | 77 | 77% |
| The Appeals Service | 15 | 60 | 95% |
| Debt Management | 15 | 35 | 100% |

* Includes a total of 2,901 letters from MPs/Peers to Ministers delegated to agency chief executives and senior business directors because they related to operational matters.

** This performance represents an improvement of four percentage points when compared to 2004.

**97** percentage of letters replied to within target.

Figure 34 **Percentage of MPs/Peers letters replied to within target since 2002**

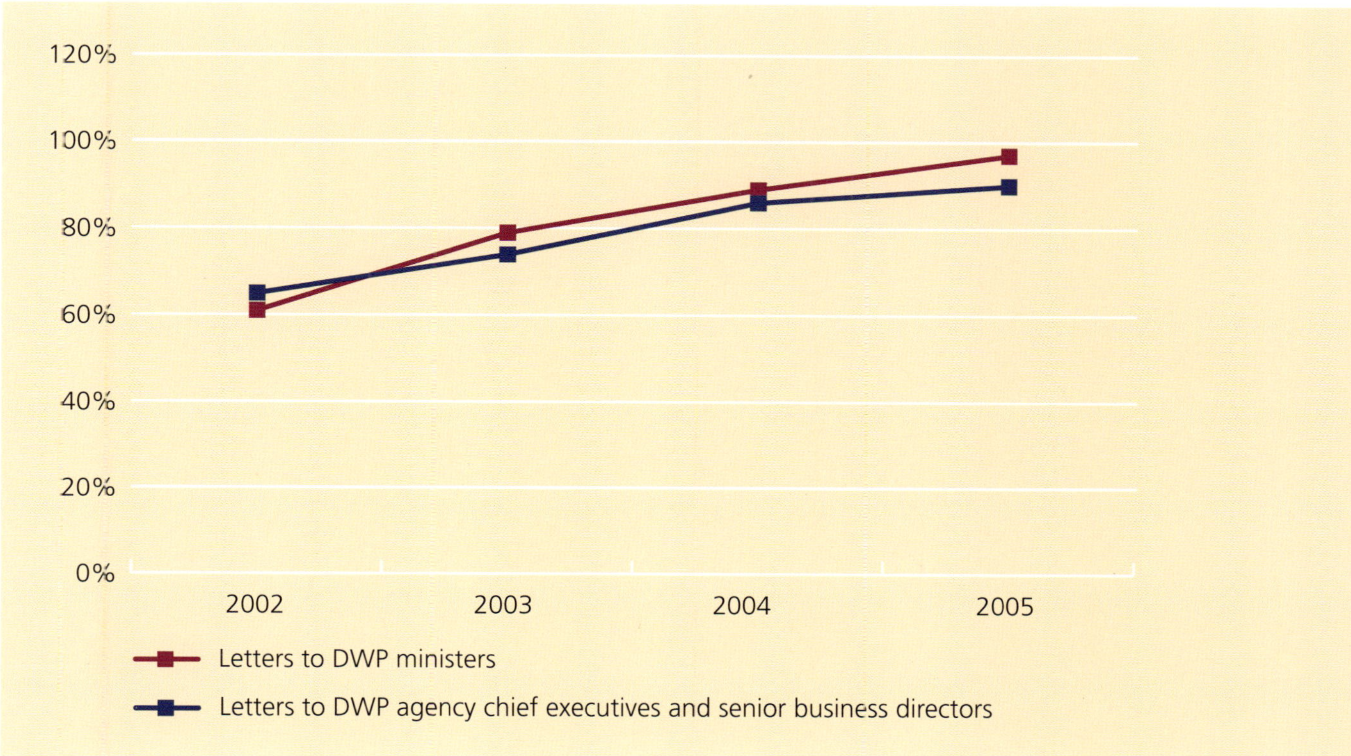


## Ministerial correspondence

### Correspondence from Members of Parliament/Peers

432. The Department's correspondence targets are:

- to respond to letters from MPs/Peers to Ministers within 20 working days; and
- to respond to letters from MP/Peers sent directly to agency chief executives and senior business directors on operational issues within 15 working days.

433. Performance against target between January and December 2005 is shown in Figure 33.

434. Figure 34 shows how performance has improved since 2002.

### Correspondence from members of the public to the Department's Ministers

435. When a member of the public writes to one of the Department's Ministers, the letter may be replied to by an appropriate official on their behalf. Figure 35 overleaf shows the volume of letters received from members of the public addressed to Ministers between January and December 2005 broken down by the drafting unit responsible for the reply and the performance achieved.

Figure 35 **Volume of letters received from members of the public addressed to Ministers between January and December 2005 and performance in replying to letters**

| | Letters received | Performance[98] |
|---|---|---|
| Ministerial Correspondence Unit/Briefing Team | 14,478 | 99% |
| Jobcentre Plus | 2,319 | 94% |
| Child Support Agency | 1,320 | 87% |
| The Pension Service | 750 | 91% |
| Disability and Carers Service | 684 | 99% |
| Debt Management | 137 | 98% |
| The Appeals Service | 32 | 93% |
| The Rent Service | 4 | 100% |
| Total | **19,724** | **97%*** |

* This performance represents an improvement of six percentage points when compared to 2004.

**98** Percentage of letters replied to in 20 working days.

## Citizen redress

436. The Department for Work and Pensions' agencies have well-developed processes for dealing with complaints, and their customer service standards and performance are described in their Annual Reports and Accounts. Details of redress arrangements are included on agency websites, and leaflets advising customers about complaints procedures are also available on request from Jobcentre Plus, Pension Centres and Disability Benefit Centres, and from local Citizens Advice Bureaux. Following the use of an impartial and independent tier for the review of complaints against the Child Support Agency, the Department began prototyping the extension of these arrangements to a sample of customers of other departmental businesses in October 2005.

437. Under a Department-wide scheme, each agency compensates any of its customers for any additional costs, losses or other effects of maladministration. In 2005–06, 41,900 ex gratia compensation awards were made under these arrangements totalling £12.3 million.

438. The Department also has procedures for handling appeals, which are clearly defined with legally agreed steps. This includes procedures for explanation and revision. Statistics on the outcome of appeals are published quarterly on the Department's website.[99]

## Communications and marketing

439. The Department's Communications Directorate advises Ministers and officials on the presentation of policy to the media and the public, and is responsible for its implementation. Marketing communications are co-ordinated and strategy prepared centrally, and delivery is undertaken centrally or by specialists within the relevant business unit. The work is funded either from the Departmental publicity budget, from project funds held by policy and operational units, or shared with other government departments.

440. 2005–06 included a number of large campaigns to inform the public about their rights and responsibilities. Each campaign delivers integrated, customer-focused material using a wide range of media. The major campaigns are listed below together with a brief description of the activity.

99 www.dwp.gov.uk/asd/recent.asp

Figure 36 **Major publicity campaigns over £500,000 during 2005–06**

| | |
|---|---|
| **Disability Discrimination Act** | **£1,446,000** |
| A campaign to increase awareness of the obligations of the DDA amongst small and medium-sized enterprises which are service providers and/or employers. It provided information on the kind of appropriate adjustments that can be considered to enable businesses to meet the needs of their disabled customers and staff. The campaign included regional press and radio advertising, supported by local PR activity. National online advertising was also used and campaign information was highlighted on the DWP web pages. | |
| **Age Positive** | **£900,000** |
| A PR campaign supported by press advertising, direct mail and exhibitions to communicate the introduction of anti-age discrimination legislation in October 2006. The Age Partnership Group is supported by a range of business stakeholders providing advice and information about the effects of the legislation and how to prepare for it. | |
| **Targeting Benefit Fraud** | **£7,587,000** |
| A campaign to deter dishonest behaviour and change attitudes towards benefit fraud. The campaign ran three times during the year and included TV, radio, regional press and outdoor advertising. It built on changes in key attitudes among customers and the general public regarding the extent and acceptability of fraud. | |
| **Winter Fuel/Age-Related Payments Campaign** | **£1,416,000** |
| A campaign to maintain the high awareness levels of Winter Fuel Payments and to build awareness and understanding of the new Age-Related Payments. It included regional and national press advertising supported by the targeted distribution of an information leaflet and poster. The messages focused on informing people of how much they were likely to receive, when they would receive it and encouraging those who need to make a claim to take action. | |
| **Pension Credit** | **£3,000,000** |
| A campaign to raise awareness and encourage customers to apply for extra money under the Pension Credit scheme. The campaign has focused mainly on one-to-one communications, with around three million direct mail shots sent to eligible pensioners. This is supported by local advertising in areas where take-up is low and by national press advertising to maintain awareness levels and further encourage customers to apply. Awareness of Pension Credit amongst the pensioner population is around 84 per cent with over 2.7 million pensioner households receiving it. | |

| Council Tax Benefit | £706,000 |
|---|---|
| A campaign to raise awareness of Council Tax Benefit among those on low income, particularly pensioners. Publicity included regional and national press advertising and insertion of a flyer into 8 million Winter Fuel Payment notification letters. Through the publicity, and by working with local authorities and other advisers, the Department aims to increase the awareness of Council Tax Benefit and in turn encourage more people on low income to claim the benefit. | |
| **Pensioners Guide** | **£1,000,000** |
| The production and distribution of a cross-government guide for pensioners on the range of help and services available to them. The guide has been promoted through GP surgeries and advertising in local newspapers. The Guide has also been sent via a direct mail campaign to pensioners, pensions advisors, and intermediaries and other professionals. It has also been produced in a range of alternative formats. | |
| **Future Pensioners/Informed Choice** | **£1,059,000** |
| Communications activity to encourage people to plan and save for their retirement, to help them understand the range of pension options available to them, and where to go for further information. This activity included the production and distribution of a series of guides on various retirement issues, mailings to members of the public and preparatory work for communications activity to take place in 2006–07 to encourage people to plan appropriately for their later life. | |
| **State Second Pension** | **£818,000** |
| A campaign using press advertising in the national and regional newspapers, women's magazines, and specialist carer and ethnic titles, along with direct mail to carer organisations. The campaign is targeted at unpaid carers and advises that if they have been looking after someone at any time during the last three years that they may be eligible for more State Pension when they retire by applying for Home Responsibilities Protection. | |
| **State Pension Deferral** | **£927,000** |
| A campaign to raise awareness of State Pension Deferral among people of working age, particularly those aged 50 and over. The campaign included advertorials in consumer magazines and ethnic press, plus online advertising, supported by paid-for editorial in regional newspapers and Direct Mail to members of the public. | |

**Notes**

1. Figures have been rounded to the best estimate at the time of going to press.
2. Some campaigns may have expenditure falling into more than one financial year, depending on the length of the campaign and the billing dates.

## Sponsorship

**441.** Government departments are required to publish details of any sponsorship exceeding £5,000 in their annual reports. During 2005–06, the Association of British Insurers sponsored an evening gala dinner at an EU UK Presidency event on 'Informed choices: retirement and savings'.

## The Department's associate bodies and public appointments

**442.** The Department sponsors a wide range of bodies to achieve its objectives; these bodies include executive, advisory and tribunal Non-Departmental Public Bodies, Public Corporations, and other arms-length and short-term bodies. Details of these bodies are available from the Cabinet Office's Agencies and Public Bodies Team website[100], and information about their remits can be found on the Department for Work and Pensions' website.[101]

**443.** The 10th report of the Committee on Standards in Public Life recommended that departments prepare an Annual Appointment Plan and adopt it as the key strategic document for each department, to set out policy and practice relating to the public appointments of chairs and board members of the public bodies they sponsor. The current Annual Appointment Plan can be found on the Department's website.[102]

## Public Accounts Committee recommendations

**444.** The Committee of Public Accounts published four reports during 2005–06, involving the Department for Work and Pensions. These were:

- 9 March 2005 – 10th Report: Welfare to Work: Tackling the barriers to the employment of older people (HC 439);
- 6 April 2005 – 27th Report: The impact of the Office of Government Commerce's initiative on the delivery of major IT-enabled projects (HC 555);
- 11 October 2005 – 4th Report: Fraud and Error in Benefit Expenditure (HC 411); and
- 15 November 2005 – 12th Report: Helping those in financial hardship: the running of the Social Fund (HC 601).
- 27 April 2006 – 36th Report: Tackling the complexity of the benefits system (HC765)

**445.** A copy of the Government responses to the above reports can be found on the Parliament website.[103]

**446.** On 29 March 2006, the Department attended a hearing before the Committee of Public Accounts entitled: 'Delivering effective services through contact centres'. The report in respect of this hearing has yet to be published.

100 www.civilservice.gov.uk/other/agencies/index.asp
101 www.dwp.gov.uk/ndpb/public_bodies.asp
102 www.dwp.gov.uk/ndpb/public_bodies.asp
103 www.official-documents.co.uk

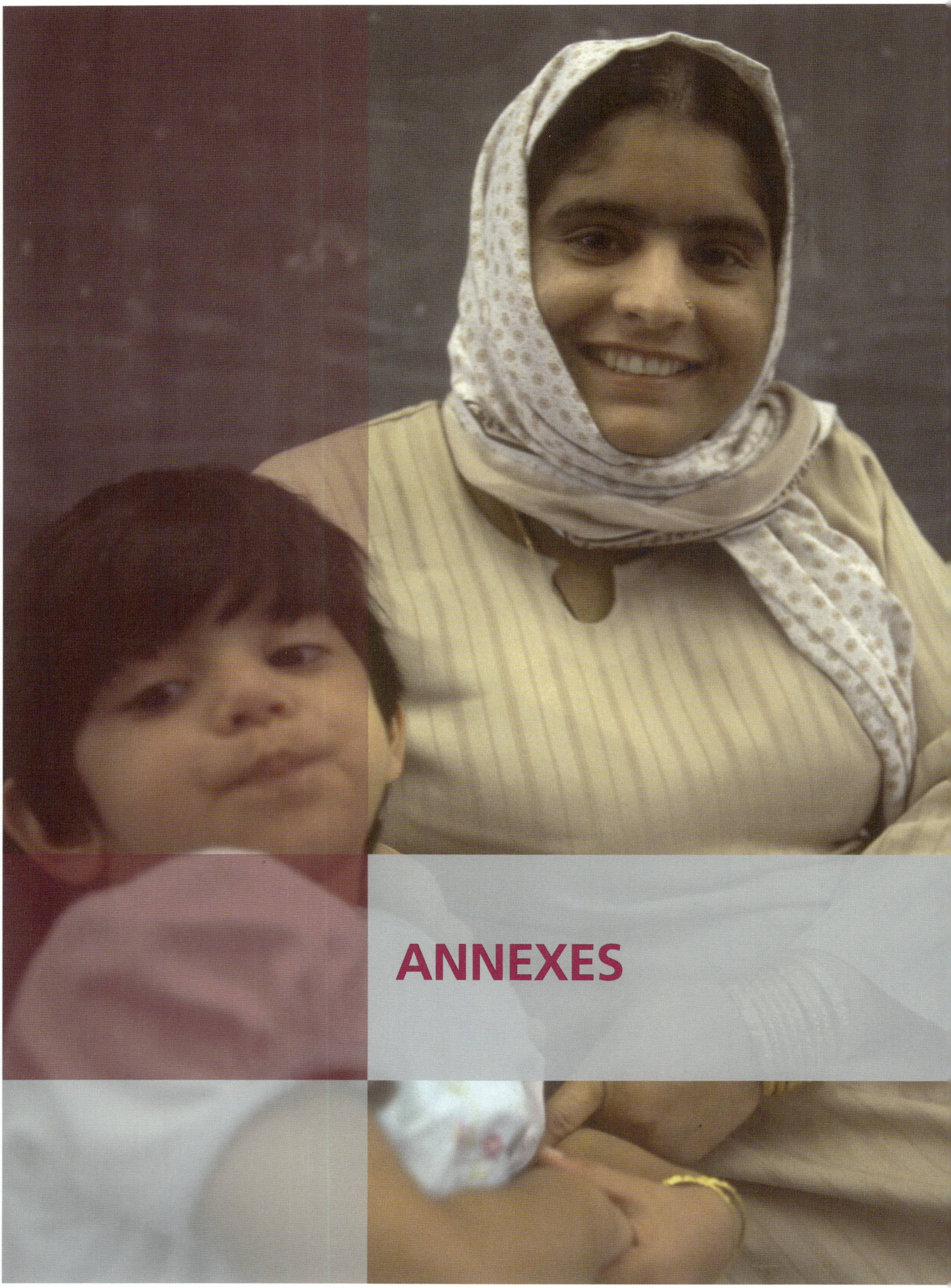

# ANNEXES

# ANNEX A EXPENDITURE TABLES

## The Government's expenditure plans 2006–07 to 2007–08

The aim of these published tables is to provide an explanation of what the Department for Work and Pensions spends money on. The tables provide an analysis of Departmental expenditure in resource terms, showing resource consumption and capital investment. The information includes Voted and non-Voted expenditure and also shows the extent to which funds are provided to support local authority activities.

## Table 1 – Department for Work and Pensions public spending

This table sets out a summary of the expenditure on functions which are now administered by the Department, covering the period from 2000–01 to 2007–08. As the Department was only formed during 2001, past years' figures have been determined on the basis of the expenditure incurred by each of the various business areas brought together by the Machinery of Government changes in June 2001. Current and future year figures reflect the budgeted figures agreed with HM Treasury for the Department as it is now, including responsibility for the Health and Safety Executive and Health and Safety Commission from 24 July 2002 and The Rent Service Executive Agency from 1 April 2004.

The table reflects the extent of the organisational changes that have taken place within the Department and presents the expenditure plans by way of the groups of clients who will be served through the consumption of the resources. The 'Corporate and shared services' grouping represents expenditure on corporate contracts, or for the provision of information technology and corporate administration. The line relating to the National Insurance Fund (NIF) represents the costs of the Department in administering contributory benefits on behalf of the NIF. These costs are met by the NIF. The consumption of resources includes both administration and programme expenditure (including benefits) where appropriate.

The capital expenditure plans are shown separately in respect of each area of administration within the Department. Expenditure by local authorities in respect of the welfare programmes is also shown on this table, and the extent to which it is supported by grants from the Department.

## Table 2 – Department for Work and Pensions resource budget detail

This table provides similar information to Table 1, though in greater detail for the resource budget. It shows the expenditure for each of the client groups, indicating the activities that the Department spends its money on. The expenditure plans differentiate between the costs of administration and expenditure incurred on the various welfare programmes. The entry concerning the National Insurance Fund relates only to the Department's costs in administering the fund.

**Table 3 – Department for Work and Pensions capital budget detail**
This table provides details of the capital expenditure plans in the same format as Table 2. Figures in respect of the Social Fund represent the level of net lending of the fund which, under Resource Accounting and Budgeting, is regarded as a capital expenditure item.

**Table 4 – Department for Work and Pensions capital employed**
This table shows the capital employed by the Department, in a balance sheet format. It provides a high-level analysis of the value of the various categories of fixed assets, debtor and creditor values, and also the extent of provisions made. The net assets of Non-Departmental Public Bodies (NDPBs) and the Public Corporation (Remploy Ltd) are shown separately.

**Table 5 – Department for Work and Pensions administration costs**
This table presents in more detail information concerning the administration costs of running the Department. For the current year and past years there is an analysis of administration expenditure showing paybill and other costs.

**Table 6 – Staff numbers 2000–01 to 2007–08**
This table shows actual and projected staffing in the Department, split between permanent staff, temporary staff and overtime. Figures for all years up to 2004–05 are based on full time equivalents and are consistent with Cabinet Office definitions at the time. Actual figures for 2005-06 are based on the Office for National Statistics specification which includes all paid staff and has the effect of increasing staff numbers by around 2 per cent. Planned figures to 2007–08 use the same specification and are based on agreed headcount plans as at 31 March 2006.

**Table 7 – Total Department for Work and Pensions identifiable expenditure on services, by country and region**
This table shows expenditure on services which can be analysed as being for the benefit of individual countries and regions. The expenditure represents the Department's total expenditure, excluding Housing Benefit and Council Tax Benefit, for each region, with country and United Kingdom totals.

The majority of the expenditure is identifiable which means that it can be recognised as having been paid to and for the advantage of individuals within particular regions. Some non-identifiable expenditure is shown from 2005–06; this is planned spending which is deemed to be on behalf of the United Kingdom as a whole.

The expenditure shown in respect of Northern Ireland and outside the United Kingdom is explained in the notes to Table 7. More information about the non-identifiable expenditure is also shown in the Table 7 notes. Expenditure plans are mostly allocated to regions on the basis of the most recent outturn information.

**Table 8 – Department for Work and Pensions identifiable expenditure on services, by country and region, per head**
This table shows expenditure on services which can be analysed as being for the benefit of individual countries and regions per head of population. This is more informative than the total expenditure information presented in Table 7, as the

size of the population varies significantly between regions. For example, while expenditure per head is highest in the North East, because it has a relatively small population, its total expenditure is the smallest of all the regions (ignoring Northern Ireland, as only a small proportion of benefit spending in Northern Ireland falls to the Department's budget).

The figures also demonstrate that expenditure per head in Wales and Scotland is consistently higher than in England, and that spending is lowest in London and the South East. The reasons for the variation in the figures are many and complex, and will depend on variations in the structure of the population and the socio-economic environment. For example, areas such as the South West with a higher proportion of pensioners will tend to show higher spending, other things being equal, while the socio-economic factors that mostly affect benefits for working-age people are discussed in detail in *Full Employment in Every Region*[112], published in December 2003 by the Department and HM Treasury.

### Table 9 – Department for Work and Pensions spending by objective by country and region in 2004–05

This table shows the expenditure for 2004–05 in Table 7 broken down into the functional categories or objectives used in Tables 1, 2, 3 and 5. The Department does not plan or allocate expenditure on a regional basis. Social security benefits are paid to eligible individuals irrespective of where they live.

### Table 10 – Expenditure on the New Deals and Action Teams

This table shows total expenditure by the Department for Work and Pensions on the New Deals and Action Teams, including expenditure funded from the Windfall Tax.

**112** www.hm-treasury.gov.uk/media/3A8/66/employment_372.pdf

Table 1 **Total public spending for the Department for Work and Pensions** **£ million (5,11)**

| | 2000–01 | 2001–02 | 2002–03 | 2003–04 | 2004–05 | 2005–06 | 2006–07 | 2007–08 |
|---|---|---|---|---|---|---|---|---|
| | outturn | outturn | outturn | outturn | outturn | estimated outturn | plans | plans |
| **Consumption of Resources:** | | | | | | | | |
| Children | 249 | 251 | 295 | 249 | 257 | 398 | 408 | 402 |
| Working age | 36,694 | 38,331 | 39,317 | 40,186 | 42,292 | 42,591 | 41,823 | 41,653 |
| Pensioners | 46,130 | 50,198 | 52,743 | 55,549 | 59,756 | 62,826 | 65,023 | 69,002 |
| Disability | 10,073 | 10,807 | 11,477 | 12,467 | 13,249 | 14,115 | 14,954 | 15,780 |
| Corporate and shared services (6) | 115 | 1,414 | 1,997 | 1,632 | 1,737 | 2,074 | 2,087 | 2,160 |
| National Insurance Fund (7) | 821 | 471 | 890 | 1,399 | 1,137 | 1,108 | 1,083 | 1,083 |
| Public corporations (12) | 100 | 143 | 113 | 108 | 109 | 3 | 92 | 92 |
| Unallocated provision | | | | | | | 168 | 245 |
| Total resource budget | 94,182 | 101,615 | 106,832 | 111,590 | 118,537 | 123,115 | 125,638 | 130,417 |
| Of which: | | | | | | | | |
| Resource DEL (1) | 5,744 | 6,057 | 6,858 | 7,650 | 7,746 | 7,935 | 7,765 | 7,699 |
| Capital spending: | | | | | | | | |
| Children | 1 | # | 1 | # | # | # | | |
| Working age | 19 | 38 | 98 | 239 | 154 | 311 | 75 | 35 |
| Pensioners (8) | 23 | 75 | 78 | 91 | 87 | 172 | 257 | 145 |
| Disability | 2 | | | 1 | 1 | 1 | | |
| Corporate and shared services (9) | 15 | 122 | 153 | -65 | 136 | 23 | 54 | 24 |
| Public corporations | | | | | | | | |
| Unallocated provision | | | | | | | | |
| Total Capital budget | 60 | 235 | 330 | 266 | 378 | 507 | 386 | 204 |
| Of which: | | | | | | | | |
| Capital DEL (2) | 37 | 161 | 253 | 175 | 298 | 406 | 178 | 63 |
| Total public spending (3,4) | 94,188 | 101,803 | 107,068 | 111,754 | 118,783 | 123,479 | 125,867 | 130,467 |

Table 1 **Continued** **£ million (5,11)**

| | 2000 –01 | 2001 –02 | 2002 –03 | 2003 –04 | 2004 –05 | 2005 –06 | 2006 –07 | 2007 –08 |
|---|---|---|---|---|---|---|---|---|
| | outturn | outturn | outturn | outturn | outturn | estimated outturn | plans | plans |
| Spending by local authorities on functions relevant to the Department (10) | | | | | | | | |
| Current Spending | 11,715 | 12,109 | 13,204 | 12,947 | 13,734 | | | |
| Of which: | | | | | | | | |
| Financed by grants from budgets, above | 11,526 | 13,638 | 14,579 | 14,348 | 16,919 | 17,984 | | |
| Capital Spending | 5 | 3 | 1 | # | # | | | |
| Of which: | | | | | | | | |
| Financed by grants from budgets, above | 11 | 6 | 8 | 8 | 3 | 3 | | |

**Further Notes**

1. Departmental Resource Expenditure Limit, set as part of the Spending Review process.
2. Departmental Capital Expenditure Limit, set as part of the Spending Review process.
3. Total public spending calculated as the total of the resource budget, less depreciation.
4. A full break down of budgets into DEL and AME voted and non-voted components is contained in the supplementary Budgetary Information publication which accompanies the Main Estimates.
5. Totals may not sum due to rounding.
6. The variation in this run of figures is mainly due to significant year by year fluctuations in modernisation expenditure, NIF receipts and re-structuring of the Department.
7. National Insurance Fund (NIF) Administration relates to the administration costs of processing NIF benefits. The variation in the NIF payment in later years partly results from a re-calculation to compensate for over/under payments in previous years.
8. Figures include net lending on the Social Fund for working age as well as pensioners. Prior to 2001-02, net lending on crisis loans and funeral payments was included under consumption of resources.
9. Negative numbers arise due to the sale of capital assets.
10. Local Authority spending is not forecast for future years.
11. Amounts below £0.5m are indicated by #.
12. Estimated outturn for Remploy grants is included within Working Age for 2005-06.

Table 2 **Resource budget for the Department for Work and Pensions** **£ million (1,2)**

| | 2000–01 outturn | 2001–02 outturn | 2002–03 outturn | 2003–04 outturn | 2004–05 outturn | 2005–06 estimated outturn | 2006–07 plans | 2007–08 plans |
|---|---|---|---|---|---|---|---|---|
| Consumption of Resources: | | | | | | | | |
| **Children** | 249 | 251 | 296 | 249 | 257 | 398 | 408 | 402 |
| of which: | | | | | | | | |
| Children's benefits | | 1 | 2 | # | | | | |
| Children's administration (3) | 249 | 250 | 294 | 249 | 257 | 398 | 408 | 402 |
| **Working age** | 36,694 | 38,331 | 39,317 | 40,187 | 42,292 | 42,591 | 41,823 | 41,654 |
| of which: | | | | | | | | |
| Working-age benefits (4,5) | 20,991 | 21,414 | 21,686 | 22,610 | 22,052 | 21,297 | 20,261 | 19,207 |
| Working-age administration (6,7) | 2,989 | 2,287 | 1,856 | 2,029 | 2,309 | 2,257 | 2,057 | 2,062 |
| Employment programmes (8) | 1,215 | 1,044 | 1,274 | 1,285 | 1,066 | 1,028 | 992 | 896 |
| Grants to local authorities | 11,462 | 13,546 | 14,460 | 14,223 | 16,825 | 17,970 | 18,479 | 19,465 |
| The Rent Service Executive Agency (9) | 37 | 40 | 41 | 40 | 40 | 39 | 34 | 24 |
| **Pensioners** | 46,131 | 50,198 | 52,743 | 55,549 | 59,756 | 62,826 | 65,023 | 69,002 |
| of which: | | | | | | | | |
| Pensioners benefits (10) | 44,262 | 48,051 | 50,478 | 53,033 | 57,089 | 60,323 | 62,491 | 66,557 |
| Social Fund (11,12) | 1,839 | 1,907 | 1,972 | 2,209 | 2,244 | 2,316 | 2,340 | 2,388 |
| Pensioners administration (13,14,15) | 30 | 240 | 293 | 307 | 423 | 187 | 192 | 57 |
| **Disability** | 10,073 | 10,807 | 11,477 | 12,467 | 13,249 | 14,115 | 14,954 | 15,780 |
| of which: | | | | | | | | |
| Disability administration (16,17) | 12 | 15 | 3 | 188 | 186 | 228 | 241 | 220 |
| Disability benefits and grants to independent bodies (18) | 10,061 | 10,792 | 11,474 | 12,279 | 13,063 | 13,887 | 14,713 | 15,560 |

Table 2 **Continued** — **£ million** [1,2]

| | 2000–01 | 2001–02 | 2002–03 | 2003–04 | 2004–05 | 2005–06 | 2006–07 | 2007–08 |
|---|---|---|---|---|---|---|---|---|
| | outturn | outturn | outturn | outturn | outturn | estimated outturn | plans | plans |
| **Corporate and shared services** | **115** | **1,414** | **1,997** | **1,632** | **1,737** | **2,074** | **2,088** | **2,160** |
| of which: | | | | | | | | |
| Corporate and shared services: administration [19] | 115 | 1,414 | 1,997 | 1,632 | 1,737 | 2,074 | 2,088 | 2,160 |
| **Public Corporations** | **100** | **143** | **113** | **108** | **109** | **3** | **92** | **92** |
| of which: | | | | | | | | |
| Remploy Ltd [7] | 100 | 143 | 113 | 108 | 109 | 3 | 92 | 92 |
| | | | | | | | | |
| **National Insurance Fund** | **821** | **471** | **890** | **1,399** | **1,137** | **1,108** | **1,083** | **1,083** |
| of which: | | | | | | | | |
| National Insurance Fund administration [20] | 821 | 471 | 890 | 1,399 | 1,137 | 1,108 | 1,083 | 1,083 |
| **Unallocated Provision** | | | | | | | **168** | **245** |
| of which: | | | | | | | | |
| Departmental Unallocated Provision | | | | | | | 38 | 105 |
| Employment Development and Skills Fund [21] | | | | | | | 40 | 50 |
| Housing Benefit Reform Fund [22] | | | | | | | 90 | 90 |
| **Total Resource Budget** | **94,182** | **101,615** | **106,832** | **111,590** | **118,537** | **123,115** | **125,638** | **130,417** |

**Further Notes**

1. Totals may not sum due to rounding.
2. Amounts below £0.5m are indicated by #.
3. Increase in 2002-03 is due to funding to implement Child Support Reform.
4. Working Age benefits include: Severe Disablement Allowance, Industrial Injuries Benefits, Income Support (under 60 years of age), Job seekers Allowance, Job Grant, Earnings Top Up, Statutory Sick Pay, Statutory Maternity Pay, Incapacity Benefit.
5. Reduction for 2005-06 onwards is a result of the transfer of child elements of income to HM Revenue & Customs.
6. Reduction for 2001-02 onwards is partly a result of the setting up of The Pension Service and the Disability Directorate, the costs of which were previously within the Benefits Agency.
7. See Note 12 in Table 1.
8. Employment Programme administration costs moved into the Working Age Administration line in 2004-05.
9. The Rent Service transferred from ODPM in April 2004.
10. Pensioner benefits mainly include: State Pension, Non-Contributory State Pension, Christmas Bonus, Pension Credit, TV Licences for the Over-75s and Widows Benefits.
11. Relates to all Social Fund resource expenditure, including Winter Fuel payments. Figures include Social Fund resource expenditure for working age as well as pensioners. From 2001-02 onwards, net lending on Crisis loans and Funeral payments was included under capital expenditure.
12. Social Fund includes Winter Fuel Payments.
13. Includes Office of the Pensions Regulatory Authority, Pensions Compensation Board and Pensions Protection Fund.
14. Increase from 2001-02 due to the setting up of the Pension Service, costs of which were previously within the Benefits Agency.
15. The reduction in 2005-06 is mainly a result of funds still to be allocated from undrawn down funds and a variation in the allocated NIF receipt.
16. Includes the Disability Rights Commission.
17. Increase from 2003-04 relates to the setting up of the Disability Directorate costs which were previously within the Benefits Agency.
18. Disability benefits include: Attendance Allowance, Disability Living Allowance, Disability Working Allowance, Invalid Care Allowance, Vaccine Damage. Grants to independent Bodies include grants to Independent Living and Motability.
19. See note 6 in Table 1.
20. See note 7 in Table 1.
21. SR2004 measure.
22. SR2004 measure.

Table 3 **Department for Work and Pensions' capital budget detail** £ million (1,2)

| | 2000–01 outturn | 2001–02 outturn | 2002–03 outturn | 2003–04 outturn | 2004–05 outturn | 2005–06 estimated outturn | 2006–07 plans | 2007–08 plans |
|---|---|---|---|---|---|---|---|---|
| Capital expenditure by activity | | | | | | | | |
| **Children** | 1 | 0 | 1 | 0 | 0 | 0 | 0 | 0 |
| Of which: | | | | | | | | |
| Children: Administration | 1 | # | 1 | # | # | # | | |
| **Working Age** | 19 | 38 | 99 | 238 | 154 | 311 | 75 | 35 |
| of which: | | | | | | | | |
| Working Age: Administration (6) | 12 | 31 | 91 | 227 | 151 | 308 | 71 | 31 |
| Employment Programmes | 3 | 2 | 6 | 6 | 2 | 3 | 4 | 4 |
| The Rent Service Executive Agency (5) | 4 | 5 | 2 | 5 | 1 | # | | |
| **Pensioners** | 22 | 75 | 78 | 91 | 87 | 172 | 257 | 145 |
| of which: | | | | | | | | |
| Social Fund (3) | 22 | 75 | 77 | 90 | 80 | 101 | 208 | 141 |
| Pensioners: Administration (7) | | | 1 | 1 | 7 | 71 | 49 | 4 |
| **Disability** | 1 | 0 | 0 | 1 | 1 | 1 | 0 | 0 |
| of which: | | | | | | | | |
| Disability: Administration | 1 | | | 1 | 1 | 1 | | |
| **Corporate and Shared Services** | 15 | 123 | 153 | -65 | 136 | 23 | 54 | 23 |
| of which: | | | | | | | | |
| Corporate Services: Administration (4) | 15 | 123 | 153 | -65 | 136 | 23 | 54 | 23 |
| **Total Capital Budget** | 60 | 235 | 330 | 266 | 378 | 507 | 386 | 204 |

**Notes**

1. Totals may not sum due to rounding.
2. Amounts below £0.5m are indicated by #
3. Relates to new net lending on Budgeting, Crisis and Funeral payments and includes expenditure on working age as well as pensioners. Prior to 2001-02, net lending on Crisis loans and Funeral payments was included under consumption of resources.
4. See Note 9 in Table 1.
5. See Note 9 in Table 2.
6. Increase from 2003-04 is a result of the Capitalisation of JC+ roll out expenditure.
7. Increase in 2005-06 and 2006-07 is a result of planned spending on the Pensions Transformation Programme.

Table 4 **Capital employed for the Department for Work and Pensions** **£ million**

| | 2000–01 outturn | 2001–02 outturn | 2002–03 outturn | 2003–04 outturn | 2004–05 outturn | 2005–06 estimated outturn | 2006–07 plans | 2007–08 plans |
|---|---|---|---|---|---|---|---|---|
| Assets on balance sheet at end of year | | | | | | | | |
| **Fixed Assets** | **261** | **406** | **549** | **610** | **767** | **945** | **1237** | **1,109** |
| Intangible Assets | 0 | 0 | 0 | 1 | 26 | 27 | 27 | 27 |
| Tangible assets of which: | | | | | | | | |
| Land and buildings | 170 | 200 | 155 | 11 | 65 | 65 | 65 | 65 |
| Leasehold Improvements (1) | 0 | 0 | 11 | 330 | 378 | 530 | 701 | 613 |
| Plant and Machinery | 3 | 9 | 8 | 6 | 6 | 6 | 3 | 2 |
| Fixtures and Fittings | 34 | 42 | 138 | 15 | 16 | 15 | 30 | 42 |
| Vehicles | 10 | 15 | 19 | 20 | 19 | 19 | 13 | 8 |
| Information Technology | 44 | 140 | 218 | 225 | 162 | 177 | 303 | 257 |
| Payments on Account & Assets under construction | 0 | 0 | 0 | 2 | 95 | 106 | 95 | 95 |
| Current Assets | 3,135 | 3,493 | 3,122 | 4,261 | 4,239 | 4,293 | 4,293 | 4,293 |
| Creditors (< 1 year) (2) | -2,996 | -3,099 | -3,245 | -3,606 | -4,600 | -3,368 | -3,368 | -3,368 |
| Creditors (> 1 year) | 0 | 0 | 0 | -274 | -340 | -283 | -283 | -283 |
| Provisions | -111 | -362 | -164 | -165 | -351 | -314 | -314 | -314 |
| **Capital employed within departmental group** | **289** | **438** | **262** | **826** | **-285** | **1,273** | **1,565** | **1,437** |
| NDPB net assets | 3 | 5 | 4 | 4 | 1 | 4 | 4 | 4 |
| Public corporation net assets | 40 | 26 | 32 | 32 | 18 | 5 | 5 | 5 |
| **Total capital employed within departmental group** | **332** | **469** | **298** | **862** | **-266** | **1,282** | **1,574** | **1,446** |

**Notes**

1. From 2003-04 the Department reviewed its accounting policy in respect of the capitalisation of expenditure on improvements to leasehold properties. As a result expenditure in respect of major capital refurbishment and improvements of properties occupied but not owned by the Department is capitalised and reported under Leasehold Improvements.
2. 2004-05 includes two exceptional items – a balance owing to the Contingencies Fund and an amount owed to paying agents.

Table 5 **Department for Work and Pensions' administration costs** £ million (1)

| | 2000–01 | 2001–02 | 2002–03 | 2003–04 | 2004–05 | 2005–06 | 2006–07 | 2007–08 |
|---|---|---|---|---|---|---|---|---|
| | outturn | outturn | outturn | outturn | outturn | estimated outturn | plans | plans |
| Administration expenditure | | | | | | | | |
| Paybill (9) | 2,364 | 2,512 | 2,850 | 2,964 | 3,076 | 3,145 | | |
| Other | 2,159 | 2,432 | 2,884 | 3,122 | 3,043 | 2,941 | | |
| **Total administration expenditure (8)** | 4,523 | 4,944 | 5,734 | 6,086 | 6,119 | 6,086 | 5,948 | 5,909 |
| Administration income | -176 | -114 | -127 | -137 | -131 | -150 | -117 | -115 |
| **Total administration budget** | 4,347 | 4,830 | 5,607 | 5,949 | 5,988 | 5,936 | 5,831 | 5,794 |
| Children | 248 | 250 | 293 | 249 | 256 | 394 | 408 | 402 |
| Working age (2) | 3,819 | 2,668 | 2,339 | 2,387 | 2,501 | 2,721 | 2,588 | 2,598 |
| Pensioners (6) | - | 219 | 419 | 484 | 571 | 623 | 641 | 507 |
| Disability (7) | - | 1 | - | 172 | 167 | 198 | 219 | 198 |
| Corporate and shared services (3,5) | 280 | 1,692 | 2,556 | 2,657 | 2,493 | 2,000 | 1,975 | 2,089 |
| **Total administration budget (4)** | 4,347 | 4,830 | 5,607 | 5,949 | 5,988 | 5,936 | 5,831 | 5,794 |

**Notes**

1. Totals may not sum due to rounding.
2 Working age includes the Employment Development Fund, Employment Development and Skills Fund and the Housing Benefit Reform Fund.
3 Corporate and shared services include the Departmental Unallocated Provision.
4 Administration costs by activity will not match the administration costs in Table 2 as the latter includes additional items outside the definition of the administration budget.
5 See Note 6 in Table 1.
6 See Notes 13 and 14 in Table 2.
7 See Note 17 in Table 2.
8 The figures in 2006–07 and 2007–08 do not agree with the Supplementary Budgetary Information publication which reports totals of £5910 million and £5805 million respectively. This is to ensure that the above table reconciles to the administration budget.
9 The actual outturn in 2005–06 is expected to show a small reduction.

Table 6 **Staff numbers 2000–01 to 2007–08 averaged over each year, showing full-time equivalent (FTE), overtime and temporary staff**

| | 2000–01 | 2001–02 | 2002–03 | 2003–04 | 2004–05 | 2005–06 | 2006–07 | 2007–08 |
|---|---|---|---|---|---|---|---|---|
| | outturn | outturn | outturn | outturn | outturn | estimated outturn | plans | plans |
| Permanent Staff | | | | | | | | |
| Children | | | 13,180 | 11,149 | 10,004 | 10,125 | 10,741 | 9,909 |
| Working age | | | 80,729 | 76,213 | 75,651 | 73,980 | 70,317 | 68,074 |
| Pensions | | | 13,330 | 18,820 | 17,250 | 15,284 | 14,550 | 12,099 |
| Disability | | | 7,225 | 7,031 | 6,658 | 6,394 | 6,160 | 5,737 |
| Corporate and shared services | | | 10,031 | 10,259 | 11,260 | 9,994 | 8,801 | 8,074 |
| Total civil service FTE | 80,935 | 117,361 | 124,495 | 123,472 | 120,823 | 115,777 | 110,569 | 103,893 |
| Overtime | 1,785 | 2,525 | 2,683 | 2,652 | 2,491 | 1,927 | 1,837 | 1,725 |
| Temporary staff | 2,145 | 4,231 | 4,231 | 4,662 | 3,674 | 2,268 | 2,110 | 1,962 |
| TOTAL | 84,865 | 124,117 | 131,409 | 130,786 | 126,988 | 119,972 | 114,516 | 107,580 |
| Information Technology Services Agency (ITSA) | | | | | | | | |
| Permanent staff | 1,879 | | | | | | | |
| Overtime | 28 | | | | | | | |
| Temporary staff | 34 | | | | | | | |
| Total ITSA | 1,941 | | | | | | | |
| | | | | | | | | |
| TOTAL DWP | 86,806 | 124,117 | 131,409 | 130,786 | 126,988 | 119,972 | 114,516 | 107,580 |

**Notes**

1. The figures for 2000-01 are the figures for the former Department of Social Security.
2. The figures for 2001–02 and future years reflect the Machinery of Government changes setting up the Department for Work and Pensions from June 2001 onwards.
3. Child Benefit Centre staff (around 2,000) transferred to HM Revenue and Customs from April 2003.
4. Figures for all years up to 2004–05 are based on full time equivalents and are consistent with Cabinet Office definitions at the time.
5. Actual figures for 2005-06 are based on the Office for National Statistics specification which includes all paid staff and has the effect of increasing staff numbers by around 2 per cent.
6. Planned figures to 2007–08 use the same specification and are based on agreed headcount plans as at 31 March 2006.

Table 7 **Department for Work and Pensions' identifiable expenditure on services, by country and region** £ million

| | 2000–01 | 2001–02 | 2002–03 | 2003–04 | 2004–05 | 2005–06 | 2006–07 | 2007–08 |
|---|---|---|---|---|---|---|---|---|
| | outturn | outturn | outturn | outturn | outturn | plans | plans | plans |
| North East | 4,534 | 4,836 | 5,016 | 5,226 | 5,369 | 5,519 | 5,588 | 5,750 |
| North West | 11,184 | 11,977 | 12,420 | 12,990 | 13,406 | 13,885 | 14,045 | 14,493 |
| Yorkshire and Humberside | 7,434 | 7,928 | 8,248 | 8,647 | 8,954 | 9,253 | 9,363 | 9,693 |
| East Midlands | 5,703 | 6,120 | 6,397 | 6,767 | 7,101 | 7,358 | 7,449 | 7,747 |
| West Midlands | 7,735 | 8,253 | 8,664 | 9,184 | 9,603 | 9,886 | 9,987 | 10,342 |
| Eastern | 6,709 | 7,204 | 7,666 | 8,159 | 8,615 | 8,919 | 9,023 | 9,403 |
| London | 8,819 | 9,348 | 9,897 | 10,622 | 11,062 | 11,134 | 11,142 | 11,422 |
| South East | 9,343 | 9,968 | 10,529 | 11,256 | 11,888 | 12,309 | 12,449 | 12,983 |
| South West | 6,817 | 7,240 | 7,594 | 8,034 | 8,423 | 8,779 | 8,902 | 9,286 |
| Total England | 68,278 | 72,874 | 76,431 | 80,884 | 84,422 | 87,042 | 87,947 | 91,119 |
| Scotland | 8,071 | 8,598 | 9,023 | 9,405 | 9,707 | 10,125 | 10,246 | 10,607 |
| Wales | 4,997 | 5,333 | 5,557 | 5,805 | 6,026 | 6,274 | 6,351 | 6,576 |
| Northern Ireland | 6 | 7 | 8 | 8 | 9 | 9 | 10 | 10 |
| Total UK identifiable expenditure | 81,352 | 86,813 | 91,019 | 96,102 | 100,163 | 103,451 | 104,553 | 108,312 |
| Outside UK | 1,537 | 1,604 | 1,692 | 1,784 | 1,963 | 1,969 | 2,055 | 2,159 |
| Total UK identifiable expenditure | 82,889 | 88,416 | 92,710 | 97,886 | 102,125 | 105,420 | 106,608 | 110,471 |
| Non-identifiable expenditure | 0 | 0 | 0 | 0 | 0 | 468 | 165 | 245 |
| Total UK identifiable expenditure | 82,889 | 88,416 | 92,710 | 97,886 | 102,125 | 105,888 | 106,773 | 110,716 |

**Notes**

1. Figures may not sum due to rounding.
2. The spending data shown in these tables is consistent with the country and regional analyses (CRA) published by HM Treasury in Chapter 7 of Public Spending Statistical Analyses (PESA) 2006. PESA contains more tables analysed by country and region, and also explains how the analysis was collected and the basis for allocating expenditure between countries and regions.
3. The tables include the spending of the department and its NDPBs on payments to private sector and subsidies to public corporations. They do not include capital finance to public corporations but do include public corporations capital expenditure. They do not include payments to local authorities or local authorities own expenditure.
4. The data are based on a subset of spending – identifiable expenditure on services – which is capable of being analysed as being for the benefit of individual countries and regions. Some planned expenditure which is incurred for the benefit of the UK as a whole, is shown as non-identifiable expenditure. The non- identifiable expenditure is made up of funding for the Departmental Unallocated Provision, Employment Development and Skills Fund, Welfare Modernisation Fund, Housing Benefit Reform Fund, Employment Development Fund and Employment Development and Modernisation Fund.
5. The tables do not include depreciation, cost of capital charges or movements in provisions that are in DEL/AME. They do include salaries, procurement expenditure, capital expenditure and grants and subsidies paid to individuals and private sector enterprises.
6. The figures were taken from the HM Treasury Public Expenditure database in December 2005 and the Regional distributions were completed in February 2006. Therefore the tables may not show the latest position and are not consistent with other tables in the report.
7. Across government, most expenditure is not planned or allocated on a regional basis. Social security payments, for example, are paid to eligible individuals irrespective of where they live; the forward plans are simply allocated on the basis of the most recent outturn data, and do not represent a regional forecast. Expenditure on other programmes is allocated by looking at how all the projects across the departments area of responsibility, usually England, compare. So the analysis shows the regional outcome of spending decisions that have on the whole not been made primarily on a regional basis.
8. The functional categories used are the same functional descriptors used in Tables 1 ,2, 3, and 5.
9. Northern Ireland expenditure relates solely to the provision of free Television Licences for those aged over 75 years of age. All other benefit expenditure in Northern Ireland is the responsibility of the Northern Ireland Social Security Agency.
10. Expenditure for outside the United Kingdom relates mainly to the payment of Retirement Pensions for older residents overseas.

Table 8 **Department for Work and Pensions' identifiable expenditure on services, by country and region per head** £ per head

| | 2000–01 | 2001–02 | 2002–03 | 2003–04 | 2004–05 | 2005–06 | 2006–07 | 2007–08 |
|---|---|---|---|---|---|---|---|---|
| | outturn | outturn | outturn | outturn | outturn | plans | plans | plans |
| North East | 1,783 | 1,904 | 1,976 | 2,058 | 2,110 | 2,180 | 2,210 | 2,276 |
| North West | 1,651 | 1,768 | 1,831 | 1,909 | 1,964 | 2,036 | 2,056 | 2,119 |
| Yorkshire and Humberside | 1,499 | 1,593 | 1,652 | 1,726 | 1,777 | 1,837 | 1,854 | 1,914 |
| East Midlands | 1,368 | 1,461 | 1,515 | 1,591 | 1,659 | 1,712 | 1,724 | 1,784 |
| West Midlands | 1,468 | 1,563 | 1,633 | 1,726 | 1,800 | 1,851 | 1,865 | 1,927 |
| Eastern | 1,248 | 1,334 | 1,414 | 1,493 | 1,569 | 1,611 | 1,619 | 1,676 |
| London | 1,219 | 1,277 | 1,343 | 1,438 | 1,489 | 1,489 | 1,481 | 1,509 |
| South East | 1,169 | 1,242 | 1,309 | 1,393 | 1,466 | 1,507 | 1,516 | 1,573 |
| South West | 1,386 | 1,465 | 1,529 | 1,607 | 1,672 | 1,734 | 1,747 | 1,810 |
| **Total England** | **1,387** | **1,474** | **1,539** | **1,622** | **1,685** | **1,732** | **1,742** | **1,797** |
| Scotland | 1,594 | 1,698 | 1,785 | 1,860 | 1,911 | 1,997 | 2,021 | 2,096 |
| Wales | 1,719 | 1,833 | 1,901 | 1,976 | 2,041 | 2,113 | 2,131 | 2,201 |
| Northern Ireland | 4 | 4 | 5 | 5 | 5 | 5 | 6 | 6 |
| **Total UK identifiable expenditure** | **1,382** | **1,469** | **1,534** | **1,614** | **1,674** | **1,723** | **1,735** | **1,791** |

**Notes**

See notes to Table 7.

Table 9 **Department for Work and Pensions' identifiable expenditure on services by function in 2004–05, by country and region**

**£ million**

| | North East | North West | Yorkshire and Humberside | East Midlands | West Midlands | Eastern | London | South East | South West | England | Scotland | Wales | Northern Ireland | UK identifiable expenditure | Outside UK | Total identifiable expenditure | Not identifiable | Total expenditure on services |
|---|---|---|---|---|---|---|---|---|---|---|---|---|---|---|---|---|---|---|
| Children | 26 | 50 | 28 | 12 | 22 | 12 | 26 | 17 | 16 | 209 | 27 | 15 | 0 | 251 | 0 | 251 | 0 | **251** |
| Working-age | 1,563 | 3,740 | 2,346 | 1,741 | 2,546 | 1,848 | 3,795 | 2,443 | 1,682 | 21,704 | 2,667 | 1,647 | 0 | 26,018 | 56 | **26,074** | 0 | **26,074** |
| Pensioners | 2,707 | 6,978 | 5,022 | 4,243 | 5,471 | 5,600 | 5,646 | 7,997 | 5,537 | 49,201 | 5,250 | 3,143 | 9 | 57,603 | 1,907 | **59,510** | 0 | **59,510** |
| Disability | 748 | 2,024 | 1,222 | 952 | 1,300 | 1,002 | 1,283 | 1,231 | 988 | 10,750 | 1,436 | 1,049 | 0 | 13,235 | 0 | **13,235** | 0 | **13,235** |
| Corporate services | 324 | 614 | 336 | 153 | 264 | 153 | 313 | 200 | 199 | 2,556 | 327 | 173 | 0 | 3,056 | 0 | **3,056** | 0 | **3,056** |
| Total | 5,368 | 13,406 | 8,954 | 7,101 | 9,603 | 8,615 | 11,063 | 11,888 | 8,422 | 84,420 | 9,707 | 6,027 | 9 | 100,163 | 1,963 | 102,126 | 0 | 102,126 |

See notes to Table 7.

Table 1C **Expenditure on the New Deals and Action Teams** **£ million**

| | 2000–01 | 2001–02 | 2002–03 | 2003–04 | 2004–05 | 2005–06 | 2006–07 | 2007–08 |
|---|---|---|---|---|---|---|---|---|
| | outturn | outturn | outturn | outturn | outturn | estimated outturn | plans | plans |
| Administrative expenditure (see notes 1–3) | | | | | | | | |
| New Deal for young people | 119 | 89 | 93 | | | | | |
| New Deal 25 plus | 18 | 73 | 71 | | | | | |
| New Deal for over 50s | 11 | 5 | 5 | | | | | |
| New Deal for lone parents | 29 | 37 | 44 | | | | | |
| New Deal for disabled people | 7 | 6 | 15 | | | | | |
| New Deal for partners | 10 | 6 | 6 | | | | | |
| Sub-total for New Deals | 194 | 216 | 234 | 111 | 113 | 121 | 125 | 129 |
| Action Teams (see note 4) | 5 | 14 | 23 | 11 | 13 | 14 | 8 | 0 |
| **Sub-total** | **199** | **230** | **256** | **122** | **126** | **135** | **132** | **129** |
| Programme expenditure (DEL) | | | | | | | | |
| New Deal for young people | 293 | 219 | 178 | 215 | 211 | 153 | 181 | 190 |
| New Deal 25 plus | 42 | 140 | 114 | 137 | 135 | 98 | 116 | 121 |
| New Deal for over 50s | 3 | 2 | 3 | 3 | 3 | 2 | 3 | 3 |
| New Deal for lone parents | 14 | 9 | 18 | 20 | 24 | 28 | 23 | 23 |
| New Deal for disabled people | 7 | 4 | 16 | 28 | 65 | 66 | 75 | 67 |
| New Deal for partners | 1 | 2 | 0 | 0 | 1 | 1 | 8 | 8 |
| Sub-total for New Deals | 360 | 376 | 328 | 404 | 439 | 348 | 406 | 412 |
| Action Teams (see note 4) | 6 | 23 | 30 | 32 | 23 | 29 | 14 | 0 |
| **Sub-total** | **366** | **399** | **358** | **437** | **462** | **377** | **420** | **412** |
| Programme expenditure (AME) | | | | | | | | |
| New Deal for young people (see note 5) | | | 43 | 49 | 43 | 43 | 44 | 46 |
| New Deal 25 plus (see note 5) | | | 53 | 52 | 44 | 44 | 41 | 45 |
| New Deal for over 50s (see note 6) | 42 | 80 | 79 | 38 | 0 | 0 | 0 | 0 |
| Sub-total | 42 | 80 | 174 | 139 | 87 | 87 | 85 | 90 |
| **Total** | **607** | **709** | **789** | **698** | **676** | **599** | **638** | **631** |

The table shows total expenditure by the Department for Work and Pensions on the New Deals and Action Teams, including expenditure funded from the Windfall Tax. All figures are rounded to the nearest £ million; totals may not sum due to rounding; expenditure of less than £500,000 shown as zero.

**Notes**

1. Following agreement with HM Treasury to remove the 'ring fences' from the New Deals in 2002–03, the Department no longer manages administrative budgets for the individual New Deals, allowing managers extended flexibility in deploying the resources available to them. Consequently information on administrative expenditure by individual New Deal is not available for 2003–04 and later years.
2. Administrative expenditure for 2002–03 is estimated.
3. Administrative expenditure for 2003–04 onwards is for staff costs only, and is not comparable to earlier years' figures which include all administrative expenditure.
4. Action Teams will come to an end in autumn 2006.
5. Allowance payments to New Deal for young people and New Deal 25 participants. Prior to 2002–03, these allowances were made from programme expenditure (DEL).
6. Subsumed within the Working Tax Credit from 2003–04.

# ANNEX B TRENDS IN BENEFIT EXPENDITURE FROM 2000–01 TO 2007–08

Figure 37 **Benefit expenditure by objective (real terms, 2006–07 prices)**

This chart shows how expenditure on benefits relates to the Department for Work and Pensions' objectives.

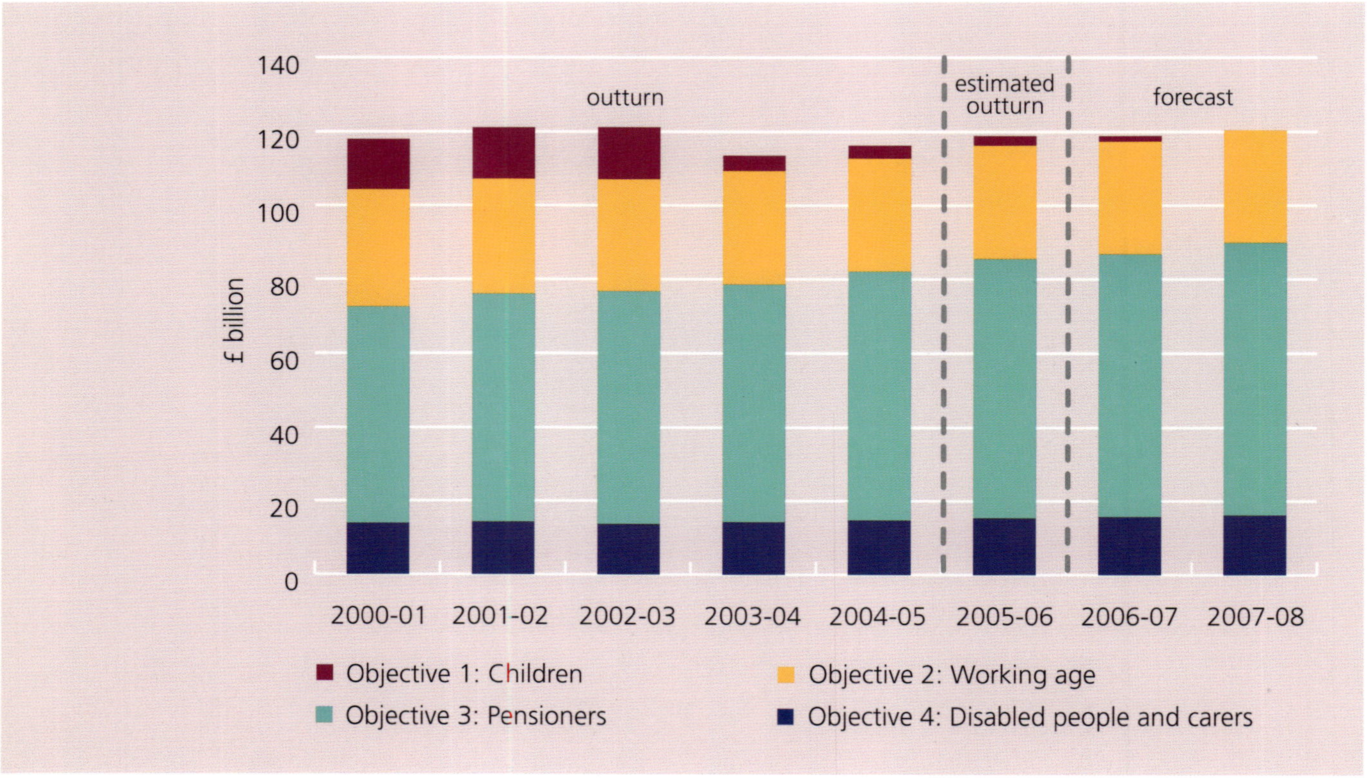


**Notes**

1 Expenditure in 2005–06 reflects the latest estimate of outturn, and not the amounts voted by Parliament.

Figure 38 **Numbers in receipt of key benefits**

This chart shows how many people receive each of seven key benefits.

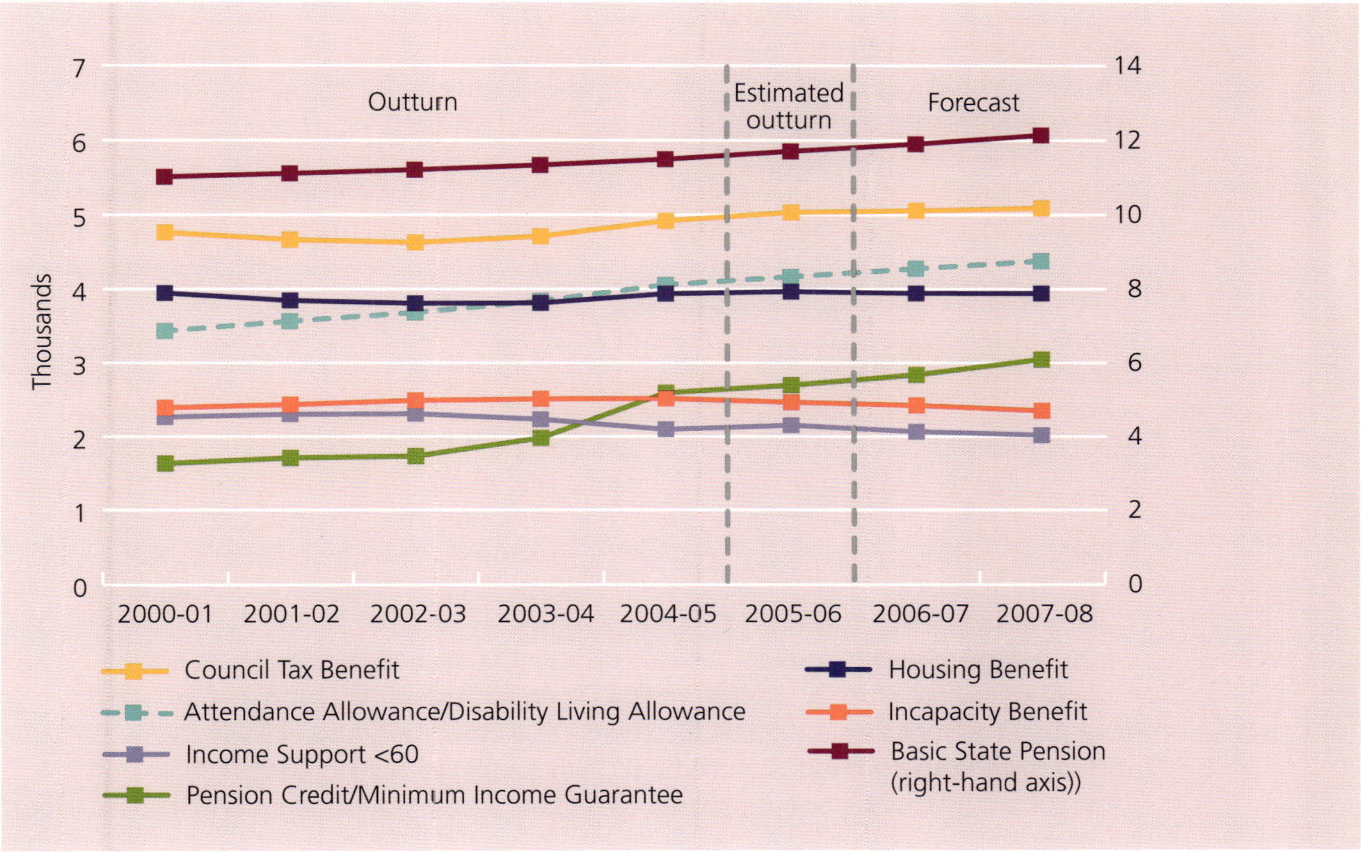


**Notes**

1 The chart shows all benefits with a caseload of at least one million in any year, except Winter Fuel Payments (where caseload is similar to Basic State Pension in all years) and free TV licences for the over-75s (where expenditure is relatively small and the main drivers are simply the cost of the TV licence and the number of people over 75).

2 Beneficiaries may receive more than one benefit at a time.

3 Incapacity Benefit includes credits-only cases. Most Incapacity Benefit credits-only cases are in receipt of Income Support.

**Analysis of benefit expenditure by Departmental objective**

All expenditure figures discussed in this section are in real terms (2006–07 prices).

Figure 37 (benefit expenditure) presents information according to the four benefit expenditure-related Departmental objectives in the Department's Public Service Agreement. Since it is possible to receive more than one benefit at a time, Figure 38 simply shows numbers of recipients for a range of key benefits.

More detail on medium- and long-term benefit expenditure is published on the Department's website at www.dwp.gov.uk/asd/asd4/expenditure.asp

## Main trends

**Slow overall growth driven by policy changes and demographics**

From the transfer of Child Benefit to HM Revenue and Customs in 2003–04 to the end of the forecast period, Department for Work and Pensions benefit spending is expected to rise by an average of less than 1 per cent a year in real terms. Growth is driven in particular by the introduction of Pension Credit in 2003–04, age-related payments in 2004–05 and 2005–06 and the extension of the payment period for maternity benefits in 2007–08. In addition, longer life-expectancy increases caseloads for pensioner benefits throughout the period.

Offsetting these effects is the transfer of Income Support and Jobseeker's Allowance child amounts to HM Revenue and Customs tax credits, with spending of £4.3 billion in 2002–03 reducing to zero in 2007–08.

Contributory benefits account for over half of the Department's benefit spending, and income-related benefits a further third. The remainder comes from non-contributory, non-income-related benefits, principally disability and carer benefits and the Winter Fuel Payment.

## Children

**Department for Work and Pensions spending falls to zero in 2007–08 as HM Revenue and Customs introduces Child Tax Credit.**

Department for Work and Pensions spending on children first fell significantly in 2003–04 with the transfer of Child Benefit (then worth nearly £10 billion in real terms) to HM Revenue and Customs. The remaining expenditure (on child elements of Income Support and Jobseeker's Allowance) is gradually migrating to Child Tax Credit, which does not feature in this report as it is administered by HM Revenue and Customs. Migration is due to be completed during 2006–07, so that the Department's spending on children is zero from 2007–08 onwards.

## People of working age

**Spending stable at just over £30 billion a year in real terms; most spending is through income-related benefits and Incapacity Benefit.**

Main reasons for benefit receipt among working-age people are unemployment, lone parenthood and sickness or disability. Although unemployment has risen recently, it is still relatively low – benefits for unemployed people account for only 13 per cent of all working-age spending in 2006–07. Lone parent benefits account for a further 23 per cent and incapacity-related benefits[113] 36 per cent. The remainder is made up principally of bereavement, carer and maternity benefits. Overall, income-related and incapacity-related benefits amount to 90 per cent of all working-age spending.

Declining caseloads in Income Support (especially lone parents) and Incapacity Benefit contribute to falling spending on these benefits in forecast years. Working-age recipients of Housing Benefit and Council Tax Benefit, too, have begun to fall, though spending is rising as rents and council tax tend to rise faster than prices.

Among the smaller benefits, Statutory Maternity Pay jumps significantly in 2007–08 as a result of extending the payment period from 26 to 39 weeks.

## People over pension age

**Increasing spending reflecting an ageing population and new spending directed at retired people; spending over £70 billion in 2006–07**

Expenditure on people over pension age is growing at 3.3 per cent a year on average over the period shown. Significant factors here have been the introduction of Pension Credit in 2003–04, and the linking of uprating to earnings rather than prices, as well as age-related payments in 2004–05 and 2005–06. In 2001–02, above-inflation uprating of the Basic State Pension – at £45 billion this year, by far the largest benefit – also contributed to growth.

Increases in the population over pension age, better contribution records for women and growing entitlements to the State Second Pension further influence the rate of growth. Overall, however, spending on people over pension age remains stable at around 6 per cent of GDP.

## Disabled people and carers

**Spending growing steadily as Disability Living Allowance progresses towards maturity; spending over £15 billion in 2006–07**

Disability and carer benefit expenditure grows by 2.3 per cent a year on average over the period shown, rising to 2.9 per cent in forecast years. The main factor is the maturing of Disability Living Allowance, where caseloads and average awards are still growing. This has a knock-on effect on the Carer's Allowance caseload, which in turn is also driven upwards by reforms including the abolition of the upper age limit for claiming the benefit.

Attendance Allowance is also growing after a period of relative stability. The impact of initiatives by The Pension Service and local authorities are believed to be factors here.

**Department for Work and Pensions benefit spending is expected to rise by an average of less than 1 per cent a year in real terms.**

**113** Incapacity Benefit, Severe Disablement Allowance and Income Support paid because of sickness or disability.

# ANNEX C **HOW THE DEPARTMENT IS ORGANISED**

The Department is organised to deliver effectively and efficiently the outcomes determined by Ministers, building on its Five Year Strategy and meeting its Public Service Agreement. The Department is structured to discharge four key roles:

- Development of department-wide strategy, planning, resource allocation and corporate policies and standards.

Identifying effective strategies, policies, resource allocation and approaches to service delivery that best meet the needs of particular client or customer groups which the Department serves.

- The direct delivery of services to meet specified customer outcomes for particular clients/customers.
- Where it is most cost-effective to do so, the procurement and/or delivery of shared services and infrastructure on a department-wide basis.

In the main, the Department's services to customers are provided by or through its executive agencies:

- **Jobcentre Plus** – helping people to find work and receive the benefits they are entitled to, and offering a dedicated service to employers to fill their vacancies quickly and successfully.
- **The Pension Service** – delivering frontline services to today's and future pensioners.
- **Child Support Agency** – administering the Child Support Scheme.
- **Disability and Carers Service** – delivering a range of benefits to disabled people and carers.
- **Appeals Service** – providing an independent tribunal body for hearing appeals.[114]
- **The Rent Service** – providing a range of advice in connection with the private rented housing sector in England.

**The Executive Team** supports the **Head of Department** in providing corporate leadership and works collaboratively to manage the Department in delivering its key objectives, ensuring that risks and opportunities are well managed. **The Departmental Board** has advisory and challenge functions. It is responsible for scrutinising, challenging and providing advice on delivery strategies, plans and programmes, performance and governance arrangements.

Additionally, policies and services to support expanding childcare and helping lone parents into work are developed by the Sure Start Unit – with joint responsibility with the Department for Education and Skills. The Department also has ministerial responsibility for the **Health and Safety Commission** and the **Health and Safety Executive**, whose mission is to protect people's health and safety by ensuring that risks in the

**114** The Appeals Service transferred to the Department for Constitutional Affairs on 1 April 2006.

changing workplace are properly controlled.

Many of the Department's services are delivered jointly with a wide range of partner organisations, for example Housing Benefit and Council Tax Benefit are administered by local authorities.

More detailed information about the structure and governance of the Department can be found in the Departmental Framework.[115]

Figure 39 **How the Department for Work and Pensions is organised**

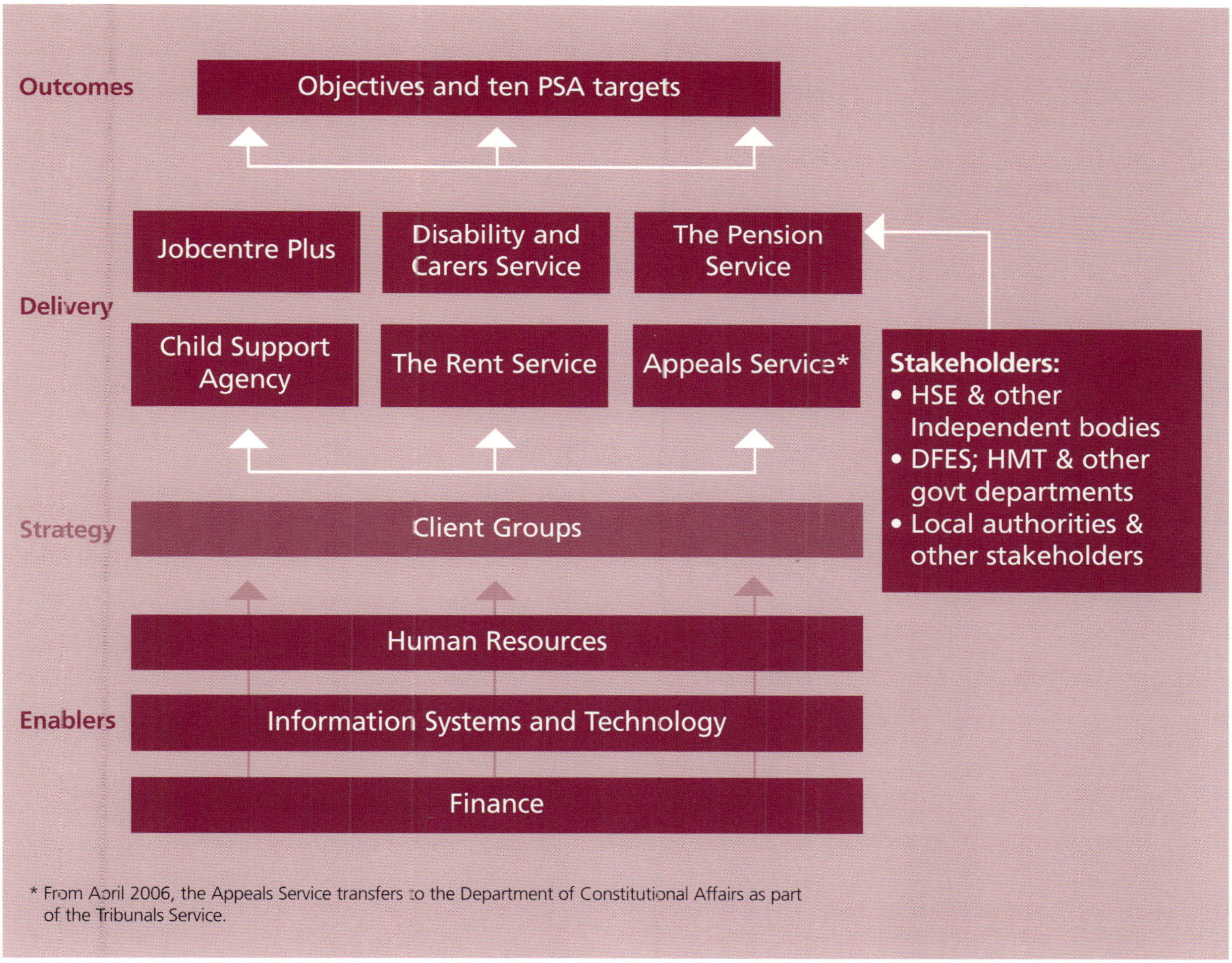


* From April 2006, the Appeals Service transfers to the Department of Constitutional Affairs as part of the Tribunals Service.

115 www.dwp.gov.uk/aboutus/dwp_framework_05 pdf

Printed in the UK for The Stationery Office Limited
on behalf of the Controller of Her Majesty's Stationery Office
ID 186611 05/06 AM4298